ENCOUNTERS WITH

JAPAN

ENCOUNTERS WITH
JAPAN

RICHARD TAMES

Foreword by Sir Peter Parker LVO

ALAN SUTTON · Stroud

ST. MARTIN'S PRESS · New York

All rights reserved. For information, write:
Scholarly and Reference Division,
St. Martin's Press · 175 Fifth Avenue
New York · NY10010

First published in the United States of America 1991

ISBN 0–312–07537–5

Library of Congress Cataloging in Publication Data applied for

First published in the United Kingdom in 1991 by
Alan Sutton Publishing · Phoenix Mill · Far Thrupp · Stroud · Gloucestershire

British Library Cataloguing in Publication Data

Tames, Richard, *1946–*
Encounters with Japan.
I. Title
952.048

ISBN 0-7509-0003-2

Typeset in Bembo 11/13.
Typesetting by Alan Sutton Publishing Limited.
Colour and duotone separation by Yeo Valley Reprographics Limited.
Printed in Great Britain
by BPCC Hazell Books, Paulton and Aylesbury

To
Marie Conte-Helm, Mavis Pilbeam and Sally Lewis

'The cherry is first among flowers, as the warrior is first among men.'

Japanese proverb

LIST OF ILLUSTRATIONS

FOREWORD

Understanding Japan is as potent a priority for the West nowadays as 'catching up with the West' once was for the Japanese. The phenomenal success of their economy has propelled what was a remote island people centre stage. That has happened so suddenly, in less than a generation. And it is even more of a shock because we were pretty certain, surely, that we had taken the measure of the place and the people. Certainly that assurance is what *Encounters with Japan* reveals in its enthralling and amusing records of visitors between 1853–1922. Actually, these were close encounters of a second kind. Richard Tames reminds us that the history of Anglo–Japanese relations is longer, more complex, darker and brighter than is generally realized.

The first close encounter was, UFO-like, in the beginning of the seventeenth century, with, of course, William Adams (now in the guise of 'Shogun', star of screen and television). The first official correspondence between us were the letters of James I and Tokugawa Ieyasu: the Shogun, well ahead of his time and perhaps ours, welcomed the possibilities of trade, but then with a characteristic touch of practicality, he admitted the awkward reality of 'the 10,000 leagues of clouds and waves between us'. By the mid-century the clouds had thickened impenetrably, the seas became a moat. Japan had slammed itself shut, the only peep-hole left was the tiny island of Deshima for Dutch traders.

For more than two hundred years the isolation continued. Then came the 'Pacific Overtures', Commander Perry's euphemism for his mission of black warships inviting Japan to join 'the civilised family of nations'. A sophisticated, compact, introverted feudal society was open to the world.

This book is a vivid mosaic of extracts from letters, newspapers, books, and the commentary by Richard Tames keeps a subtle balance between the curious and the serious. The challenge of not being patronizing with hindsight is one he can cope with, he has the wit and erudition – and the love. Love is crucial. The great Basil Chamberlain held Lafcadio Hearn better than any other interpreter of Japan 'because he loves it better'.

I have to say that love does not abound in many of the Victorian and Edwardian observations. Some are genial enough, some generous, some amusing, some scornful, a very few prescient – nearly all patronizing. A sense of superiority is the common denominator. Not only the professional writers but also the professional military observers missed the target. Japanese troops, it seemed, could not stand up to European troops 'as its men lack the true military instincts'. Even the sensible Major Knollys, who gave Japanese troops top marks for good behaviour, ends up implying their discipline is docility: 'Better surely that he should occasionally insult his sergeant-major'. They lacked 'the spirited impetuosity of a proper soldier'.

It was the cooler Gallic view that had more of the future in it – General Descharmes who discussed 'le diable dans le corps for fighting'. He would not contemplate landing an army in Japan 'with less than 60,000 men, all Frenchmen'.

With hindsight, that most accurate type of vision, it is obvious that nobody was able to foretell the astounding destiny for the land of the beautiful and the useful. At best, a few sensed the tension at the heart of all the changes afoot, the bewildering resolve of Japan to keep itself to itself and yet go flat out for westernization.

It is this immanence of things to come which gives the book its fascination and significance. There is much more to it than the self satisfaction of feeling superior with our historical advantage. I find myself struck by two aspects of these annals. First, we learn so much more about ourselves by what we say of others. These assessments of discoverers of Japan say so much about the British. The enduring popularity of *The Mikado* by Gilbert and Sullivan depends, as Tames reminds us, not on 'its painstaking, but entirely superficial Japaneseness, but on its Englishness'. The jokes in the musical comedy were all against the English, not against the Japanese. G.K. Chesterton pointed out there is much good humour in the British reaction to Japan, but much danger too. With all the immense interest in things Japanese we were too quick to settle on first impressions. The *Daily Telegraph* felt in the 1880s that 'we are all being more or less Japaned now'. The exhibition in 1910 in White City attracted six million visitors, but still what Richard Tames calls 'superficial Japaneseness' remains a serious charge against us at our end of the Anglo–Japanese relationship. There is a similarity: the Japanese have a greater knowledge of Britain than we have of them. The gap between the expert Japanophiles and the general knowledge of Japan, even among educated Westerners, is an aching void. The historical reasons are obvious, and Tames reflects them wonderfully. The Japanese were determined to catch up with us. But naturally enough we saw the relationship differently. I experienced a moment which symbolized the difference: my wife and I were taken by an old friend to the Foreigners Cemetery at Yokohama; Jill was presented with bouquets to put on the graves of two young Great Western Railway engineers who had worked themselves to death to start up the railways in Japan. The Japanese have taken the British seriously from the start. Truly we have only recently begun to take the Japanese seriously, and that has been happening during the close encounters of the third kind with modern Japan, in war and in peace.

This remarkable book reminds us, however, of prominent themes in the Anglo–Japanese relationship: the search for better understanding between us, the importance of the frankness of friendship, and above all of keeping friendships in good repair. My hope is that Westerners will learn more about modern Japan, how it happened and how it sees its future in the world. And in this enjoyable process I hope there will be opportunities for more close encounters, but this time of a fourth kind. I hope it will take us forward beyond a festival culture into a robust and normal alliance between the Japanese and English speaking world. Richard Tames' fresh presentation of the past gives us just the perspective that will help with advance.

Sir Peter Parker LVO

INTRODUCTION

'. . . the king demanded of me, of what land I was, and what moved us to come to his land, being far off. I showed unto him the name of our country, and that our land had long sought out the East Indies, and desired friendship with all kings and potentates in way of merchandise . . . Then he asked whether our country had wars? I answered him yea, with the Spaniards and Portugals. He asked me in what did I believe? I said, in God, that made heaven and earth. He asked me divers others questions of things of my religion, and many other things – as what way we came to the country. Having a chart of the whole world I showed him, through the Strait of Magellan. At which he wondered and thought me to lie. Thus, from one thing to another, I abode with him till midnight . . . In the end, he being ready to depart, I desired that we might have trade of merchandise, as the Portugals and Spaniards had. To which he made me an answer, but what it was, I did not understand . . .'

So ended the first recorded encounter between Japan and the English-speaking world. The 'king' in question was Tokugawa Ieyasu, who established the dynasty of *shoguns* (military dictators) which ruled Japan in the name of its emperor from 1603 to 1867. The narrator was William Adams, the first Englishman to reach Japan and the only foreigner ever to achieve the unique distinction of becoming a samurai. The year was 1600.

The encounter between these two men, a rising warlord and a shipwrecked pilot, foreshadows many of the themes which are the concern of this book – Japanese curiosity about the outside world, western interest in the commercial potential of Japan and the impulse on both sides to broaden the encounter and range from one topic to another, from politics to religion, from trade to technology. Language was certainly a barrier to this particular exchange (conducted through a Portuguese Jesuit interpreter), but two other major barriers seem to have been absent – prejudice and preconception. The fact that the one party was completely at the mercy of the other (and both knew it) may help to explain this. The terms of exchange in subsequent encounters were far less clear, with results that should be apparent throughout this book.

Direct contact between Japan and the English-speaking world ended with the closure of the East India Company's Japanese trading-base in 1623. It was not to be successfully renewed until the arrival in 1853 of the American naval force, commanded by Commodore Perry, which forced the Japanese to end the policy of isolation initiated by the Tokugawa shoguns to seal the country from the disturbing influences of Christian missionaries and would-be conquerors. For over two centuries contact with the West was limited to a trickle of trade conducted through Dutch

merchants who were kept firmly in their place – a small island in Nagasaki harbour. Economically and ecologically – but not entirely culturally or technologically – Japan was a closed system.

'Old Japan was an oyster – to open it was to kill it.' – thus Basil Hall Chamberlain, British diplomat, and with his colleagues, Ernest Satow, W.G. Aston and A.B. Mitford, one of the founders of 'Japanology', the attempt to explain Japan to the West and, initially at least, to no little extent, to the Japanese themselves as well. The death of 'Old Japan' cannot be separated from what contemporaries almost unanimously realized was the birth of a 'New

Japan'. Chamberlain elegantly expressed, in the Introduction to his brilliant vade-mecum *Things Japanese*, the wonderment of those who lived through this process:

> To have lived through the transition stage of modern Japan makes a man feel preternaturally old; for here he is in modern times, with the air full of talk of bicycles and bacilli . . . and yet he can himself distinctly remember the Middle Ages. The dear old Samurai who first initiated the present writer into the mysteries of the Japanese language, wore a queue and two swords . . . His modern successor, fairly fluent in English . . . might almost be a European, save for a certain obliqueness of the eyes and scantiness of beard. Old things pass away between a night and a morning. The Japanese boast that they have done in

thirty years what it took Europe half as many centuries to accomplish. Some even go further, and twit us Westerns with falling behind in the race.

With more than a hint of regret Chamberlain observed that:-

Antiquated persons doubtless exist here and there to whom Buddhist piety is precious; others may still secretly cherish the swords bequeathed to them by their knightly forefathers; quite a little coterie has taken up with art; and there are those who practise the tea ceremonies, arrange flowers according to the traditional esthetic rules, and even perform the mediaeval lyric dramas. But all this is merely a backwater. Speaking generally, the educated Japanese have done with their past. They want to be somebody else and something else than what they have been and still partly are.

Chamberlain was, perhaps, unusually aware that the collision of east and west had occasioned a situation in which 'culture shock' was mutual:

. . . our European world of thought, of enterprise, of colossal scientific achievement, has been as much a wonder-world to the Japanese as Old Japan could ever be to us . . . Old Japan was to us a delicate little wonder-world of sylphs and fairies. Europe and America, with their railways, their telegraphs, their gigantic commerce, their gigantic armies and navies, their endless applied arts founded on chemistry and mathematics, were to the Japanese a wonder-world of irresistible genii and magicians.

But Chamberlain, however, realized that, no matter how eager the Japanese were to 'westernize', they were by no means uncritical in their admiration of the West:

. . . the travelled Japanese consider our three most prominent characteristics to be dirt, laziness and superstition . . . Europe and America make a far less favourable impression on the Japanese visitor than seems to be generally expected. Be he statesman or be he valet, he is apt to return to his native land more patriotic than he left it.

And as for 'Old Japan', Chamberlain wryly proposed his own formula for 'encounter':

Feudalism has gone, isolation has gone, beliefs have been shattered, new idols have been set up, new and pressing needs have arisen. In the place of chivalry there is industrialism, in the place of a small class of aristocratic native connoisseurs there is a huge and hugely ignorant foreign public to satisfy . . . Old Japan is dead, and the only decent thing to do with the corpse is to bury it. Then you can set up a monument over it, and, if you like, come and worship from time to time at the grave; for that would be quite 'Japanesey'.

A permanent diplomatic and mercantile community, improved steamship services and the opening of the Suez Canal in 1869 all conspired to bring a host of westerners to Japan, for periods varying from a few days to half a lifetime. Many felt compelled to record their impressions for the benefit of their curious countrymen. Chamberlain himself humorously noted of this phenomenon:

> The late Mr. Gifford Palgrave said, in the present writer's hearing, that an eight weeks' residence was the precise time qualifying an intelligent man to write about Japan. A briefer period (such was his ruling) was sure to produce superficiality, while a longer period induced a wrong mental focus. By a curious coincidence, eight weeks was the exact space of time during which that brilliant conversationalist and writer had been in Japan when he delivered himself of this oracle.

A century later that talented journalist James Cameron confessed that the enchantment was still as strong as ever:

> Japan has the instant effect upon me of making it imperative to write of it . . . as though it had not in fact been done a hundred times before, as though oneself was the first to be beguiled by the subtle flavour of the place. Just a little more study, I felt, just the experience of one more month and it could be done. Of course it never will.

The main focus of this book lies, therefore, in the half century or so after the forced opening of 1853. Fifteen years of exciting and violent political confusion issued in a brief civil war which led the new regime, ruling under the aegis of the young emperor 'Meiji', to launch – after some hesitation – a programme of modernization to enable Japan to 'catch up' with the West. Technical, administrative and other experts from English-speaking countries played a leading role in this process, for Britain and America were Japan's most important models of what a modern country should be.

What follows is only a very brief and, no doubt, idiosyncratic selection from an immense, diverse and hugely entertaining literature. Those who are beguiled to go further may find a serviceable starting-point in the suggestions for further reading appended at the end of the book.

Richard Tames

Characteristic subject matter for the enthusiastic Victorian photographer. The factories and railways in which the Japanese themselves took pride were invariably ignored

ENCOUNTERS WITH JAPAN

The 'Commander-in-Chief US Naval Forces, East India, China and Japan Seas, and Special Ambassador to Japan' was known to his men as 'Old Bruin' and to history as Commodore Matthew Calbraith Perry. The purposes and methods of his celebrated expedition were outlined by the US government as follows:

Since the islands of Japan were first visited by Europeans, efforts have constantly been made by the various maritime powers to establish commercial intercourse with a country whose large population and reputed wealth hold out great temptations to mercantile enterprise. Portugal was the first to make the attempt, and her example was followed by Holland, England, Spain, and Russia; and finally by the United States. All these attempts, however, have thus far been unsuccessful; the permission enjoyed for a short period by the Portuguese to trade with the islands, and that granted to Holland to send annually a single vessel to the port of Nagasaki, hardly deserving to be considered exceptions to this remark . . .

So rigorously is this system of exclusion carried out, that foreign vessels are not permitted to enter their ports in distress or even to do an act of kindness to their own people . . .

Every nation has undoubtedly the right to determine for itself the extent to which it will hold intercourse with other nations. The same law of nations, however, which protects a nation in the exercise of this right imposes upon her certain duties which she cannot justly disregard. Among these duties none is more imperative than that which requires her to succour and relieve those persons who are cast by the perils of the ocean upon her shores . . .

That the civilized nations of the world should for ages have submitted to such treatment by a weak and semi-barbarous people, can only be accounted for on the supposition that, from the remoteness of the country, instances of such treatment were of rare occurrence, and the difficulty of chastising it very great . . .

The objects sought by this government are –

1. To effect some permanent arrangement for the protection of American seamen and property wrecked on these islands, or driven into their ports by stress or weather.

2. The permission to American vessels to enter one or more of their ports in order to obtain supplies of provisions, water, fuel &c., or, in case of disasters, to refit so as to enable them to prosecute their voyage.

3. The permission to our vessels to enter one or more of

Reflections

their ports for the purpose of disposing of their cargoes by sale or barter . . .

It is manifest, from past experience, that arguments or persuasion addressed to this people, unless they be seconded by some imposing manifestation of power, will be utterly unavailing.

. . . If, after having exhausted every argument and every means of persuasion the commodore should fail to obtain from the government any relaxation of their system of exclusion . . . he will then change his tone . . .

According to Perry's official chronicler, Francis Hawks, the appearance of a US naval squadron in Japanese waters on 8 July 1853 impelled local fishermen to flee for the shore 'like wild birds at a sudden intruder.' Providence then handily arranged the passage of a flaming comet that night, which surely should have impressed upon the Japanese that Perry was no ordinary emissary to be turned away with fair words. Perry himself is said to have suggested that the heavenly portent:

. . . may be so construed by us, as we pray for God, that our present attempt to bring a singular and isolated people into the family of civilized nations may succeed without resort to bloodshed.

Implicit in this piety was the clear threat that bloodshed would indeed to resorted to should it prove necessary. But first the Commodore would try swagger. When he finally deigned to go ashore Perry was matched step for step by two huge black sailors – 'two of the best-looking fellows of their colour that the squadron could furnish' – plus an escort of marines and a very noisy band. 'And all this parade was but for effect.' Having presented their demands, the Americans sailed away, promising to return the following year for an answer. They came back, as promised, with gifts – and twice as many ships.

The most spectacular gift was a miniature railway with 350 ft of 18-in gauge track. Hawks' amused account makes it clear that it was a great success:

It was a spectacle not a little ludicrous to behold a dignified mandarin whirling around a circular road at a rate of twenty miles per hour with his loose robes flying in the wind. As he clung with a desperate hold to the edge of the roof, grinning with intense interest and his huddled-up body shaking convulsively with a kind of laughing timidity while the car spun rapidly round the circle, you might have supposed that the movement somehow or other was dependent rather upon the enormous exertion of the uneasy mandarin than upon the power of the little puffing locomotive which was easily performing its work.'

The complete list of gifts intended for the Emperor provides an intriguing illustration of what the Americans believed to represent their culture at its best:

One ¼ size miniature steam engine, track, tender and car.
Telegraph, with three miles of wire . . .
One Francis' copper life boat.
One surf-boat of copper.
Collection of agricultural implements.
Audubon's Birds, in nine vols.
Natural History of the State of New York, 16 vols.
Annals of Congress, 4 vols.
Laws and Documents of the State of New York.
Journal of the Senate and Assembly of New York.
Lighthouse Reports, 2 vols.
Bancroft's History of the United States, 4 vols.
Farmers' Guide, 2 vols.
One series of United States Coast Survey Charts.
Morris' Engineering.
Silver-topped dressing case.
8 yards scarlet broadcloth, and ps. scarlet velvet.
Series of United States standard yard, gallon, bushel, balances and weights.
Quarter cask of Madeira.

European-style castles appeared in the late sixteenth century together with cannons and firearms

Barrel of whiskey.
Box of champagne and cherry cordial and maraschino.
Three 10 cent boxes of fine tea.
Maps of several states and four large lithographs.
Telescope and stand in box.
Sheet-iron stove.
An assortment of fine perfumery, about 6 dozen.
5 Hall's Rifles, 3 Maynard's Muskets, 12 Cavalry
    Swords, 6 Artillery Swords, 1 Carbine and 20 Army
    Pistols in a box.
Catalogue of New York State Library and of Post-
    offices.
Two mail bags with padlocks.

The Empress had to make do with:

Flowered silk embroidered dress.
Toilet dressing-box gilded.
6 dozen assorted perfumery.

*Japanese officials received gifts graded according to their perceived
seniority. But all of them appear to have been presented with
those crucial products of western civilization – a clock, a sword, a
rifle, a revolver and at least five gallons of whisky.*

    *In return the Americans received an assortment of bronzes,
lacquer-ware, umbrellas, paper, ceramics, bamboo goods and fine
textiles. They were unimpressed:*

A poor display, not worth over a thousand dollars some
thought . . . our railroad engine and car cost several times
their total value.

*To underline the impression of American superiority Perry
invited senior Japanese officals aboard one of his ships for a
demonstration of its fighting prowess:*

. . . we amused them with an exercise of our Great Guns
and small arms, showing them how we boarded an enemy
and how we repulsed one attempting to board . . .

This was followed by a lavish disbursement of naval hospitality:

. . . in obedience to orders, I plied the Japanese in my
neighbourhood well, and when clean work had been made
of champagne, Madeira, cherry cordial, punch and whisky

Pagoda at the Horyuji temple complex, the oldest surviving group of wooden buildings in the world, dating from the eighth century

I resorted to . . . a mixture of catsup and vinegar which they seemed to relish with equal gusto.

To complete their entertainment the Americans then mounted an impromptu 'nigger minstrel' show. What the Japanese thought of this final proof of the advanced state of American culture is not recorded.

Nevertheless Perry got his treaty and at least one of his retinue recognized that he had pulled off quite a coup:

. . . the military and warlike strength of the Japanese had long been to Europe like the ghost in a village churchyard, a bugbear and a terror which it only required some bolder fellow than the rest – like we Yankees – to walk up and discover the ghost to be nothing but moonshine on the gravestones . . . Our nation has unclothed the ghost and all the rest of the world will cry 'bah' and take advantage of the discovery.

America's first permanent diplomatic representative in Japan was Townsend Harris, who, although a much-travelled businessman, was without diplomatic experience or even a university education. In petitioning the President for the position of Consul-General, Harris argued that he had the most essential qualification for the job in being:

. . . a single man, without any ties to cause me to look anxiously to my old home, or to become impatient in my new one . . . I have a perfect knowledge of the social banishment I must endure while in Japan and the mental banishment in which I must live and I am prepared to meet it.

In August 1856 Harris confided to his journal:

I hope I may so conduct myself that I may have honorable mention in the histories which will be written on Japan and its future destiny.

A month later Harris took up residence in an abandoned temple at Shimoda and, having hoisted the Stars and Stripes, noted enigmatically:

Grim reflections – ominous of change – undoubted beginning of the end. Query: if for the real good of Japan?

Although he had a cheerful young Dutchman, Heusken, as a companion and interpreter, Harris found that his premonitions of isolation were all too accurate:

Merry Christmas! How happy are those who live in lands where these joyous greetings can be exchanged! As for me, I am sick and solitary, living as one may say in a prison – a large one it is true – but still a prison.

Throughout the months that followed Harris negotiated tirelessly with Japanese officials, hammering out detailed procedures for the conduct of trade and treatment of foreign residents. It was a wearisome business:

Travelled over the debates of yesterday like a horse in a mill . . . I am really ill, yet I am forced day after day to listen to useless debates on points that have been exhausted and only varied by some new phase of falsehood.

Even when his dogged persistence ultimately paid off Harris was little gratified:

Am I elated by this success? Not a whit. I know my dear countrymen but too well to expect any praise for what I have done, and I shall esteem myself lucky if I am not removed from office, not for what I have done, but because I have not made a commercial treaty that would open Japan as freely as England is open to us.

He was, furthermore, dogged by persistent illness:

Jan 15 1857.

Ill, ill, ill, I am constantly wasting away in flesh. I am most careful in my diet, but all is of no avail. What it is that ails me, I cannot say.

April 18 1857.

My health is not good. I wish the frigate would arrive, that I could have some medical advice.

June 23 1857.

My health is miserable. My appetite is gone and I am so shrunk away . . .

July 4 1857.

I never felt more miserable and wretched than this day. Ill in health and in want of everything but low spirits, of which I have an abundant supply.

In November 1857 Harris passed a diplomatic milestone, becoming the first representative of a foreign power to have an audience with the shogun. He was entirely aware of the significance of this unspectacular event:

Today I am to enter Yedo (Tokyo). It will form an important epoch in my life, and a still more important one in the history of Japan.

When it came to the actual presentation Harris was determined to be appropriately resplendent. His Paris-made uniform had been designed by himself:

My dress was a coat embroidered with gold . . . blue pantaloons with a broad gold band running down each leg, cocked hat with gold tassels and a pearl handled dress sword.

(Reports of Harris' self-styled splendour eventually caused the US State Department to tighten up its dress regulations in favour of a more seemly republican sobriety.)
The 'Embassador Merrican' received a curt but not unpromising response to his representations:

Pleased with the letter sent with the Ambassador from a far distant country, and likewise pleased with his discourse. Intercourse shall be continued forever.

Harris' successful audience was followed by months of further tedious nit-picking over technicalities, accompanied by a serious illness, which brought him to death's door. Heusken was frantic:

His body is . . . covered with purple spots . . . and they say . . . it is impossible to save him . . . What am I to do? My God! This is a terrible thing.

The indomitable Harris pulled through, however, and served for

another three years before returning to a comfortable, if obscure, retirement in New York.

Thanks to the groundwork done by Townsend Harris – and the kindly loan of Heusken's services as interpreter – the British mission headed by His Excellency the Earl of Elgin and Kincardine, which arrived in 1858, was able to conclude a treaty with the Japanese in a couple of weeks. Liberal dispensations of champagne and foie gras may also have helped jolly things along. The eminently civilized Elgin was a man who deplored aggression and bombast and regretted that he found so much of Asia:

. . . strewed all over with records of our violence and fraud and disregard of right . . . I have seldom from man or woman since I came to the East, heard a sentence which was reconcilable with the hypothesis that Christianity had ever come into the world.

Despite its leader's sensitivity Elgin's mission did blunder in at least one respect. Perhaps in an effort to outbid Perry's model steam locomotive, Her Majesty's Government had sent with its envoy an even more extravagant present for the shogun – a 300-ton steam yacht. As the shogun was virtually a prisoner in his own palace the gift was, as Laurence Oliphant, Elgin's witty secretary, observed, perhaps not the most appropriate choice:

It was a cruel satire upon this unhappy potentate to present him with a yacht; one might as well request the Pope's acceptance of a wife.

That aside, Elgin did steam away with the treaty in his pocket and every reason for feeling pleased with himself. It is perhaps unsurprising that he concluded that:

The Japanese are the nicest people possible.

'. . . if Japanese writing is a mountain of difficulty, it is unapproachably beautiful . . . in comparison with it, the freest, boldest English hand is little better than the cramped scribble of some rheumatic crone.'

Basil Hall Chamberlain

Silver Pavilion, Kyoto

But, then, he only stayed for a fortnight.

Britain's first permanent diplomatic representative in Japan was Sir Rutherford Alcock, an army surgeon turned diplomat, who had successfully brought some sort of order to the booming city of Shanghai and turned to the task of establishing an official British presence in Japan brimming with self-confidence.

Alcock's account of his tour of duty – The Capital of the Tycoon *– is important because, being based on the first-hand experiences of a hyperactive diplomat, it was long held in great esteem. A.B. Mitford – who was far to surpass Alcock in expert knowledge of Japan – observed sourly that his chief:*

. . . [would] have been a greater man if he had never written a book about a country which he did not understand, or a grammar of a language which he could neither read nor write.

The fact that Mitford had served the ebullient Alcock in the office of amanuensis may no doubt have coloured his judgement a little:

. . . to copy these effusions with the thermometer at 108 in the shade, with a double sheet of blotting paper between my hand and the foolscap and a basin of water to dip my fingers in from time to time, was like being private secretary to Satan in the nethermost regions.

Like Townsend Harris, Alcock experienced intense loneliness, despite the fact that he had not one companion but at least five:

As a man never feels more alone than when the sense of loneliness comes upon him in a crowd . . . in this wilderness of living men the foreigner is too entirely a stranger and too absolutely repudiated as having anything in common with the natives, to feel otherwise than banished and exiled from all social intercourse.

Companionship was not all he missed:

Pork and tough fowls for meat, and rice for vegetables, eggs for milk (butter and milk being both unknown luxuries here), with an occasional pigeon for entremet, may support life even under the barbarous handling of a Japanese or Chinese cook – twin brothers in capacity and instinct; but I am satisfied there must be a limit somewhere . . . The total deprivation of beef and mutton must in time be a serious detriment to the English constitution . . .

Alcock established himself in the beautiful Tozenji temple and set himself to produce an English – Japanese grammar. He soon discovered that the Japanese language harboured horrors unsuspected. Even a seemingly straightforward matter like the numbering system appeared, upon investigation, to exhibit the most bizarre complexities:

There is one class of numerals for all animals – except the flying and swimming species, and insects. Another for birds, in which, however, hare and rabbits are included!

And as for verbs:

. . . my despair may be conceived when, as a mere tyro and foreigner, I came to the task of unravelling their intricacies, and digging beneath the surface, overlaid with distinctions, for the simple elements and roots. Many times I was more than half disposed to give up the undertaking in utter hopelessness of ever seeing my way to any useful end.

Alcock's grammar proved to be a labour in vain as it was soon to be replaced by the work of more expert linguists. More lasting in value (though it added even less to his reputation) was his attempt to lay down:

Rules and Regulations for the Peace, Order and Good Government of British Subjects within the Dominions of the Tycoon of Japan.

Having cleaned up Shanghai, Alcock was eager to stop the new trading settlement at Yokohama getting out of hand, requiring its foreign inhabitants to observe a speed limit and rules of the road and to refrain from discharging firearms in public places.

Although firing guns might be regarded as anti-social, carrying one was simply a sensible precaution. Many samurai were bitterly opposed to the government's abandonment of isolation and resented the influx of aliens. Alcock's own Japanese interpreter was stabbed to death at the very entrance to the British Legation and the popular young Dutchman, Heusken, was hacked down one night riding back from a visit to the Prussian Legation. Alcock's fury and frustration can be sensed from his description of Heusken's funeral:

The beauty of the site and clearness of the sky only contrasted the more painfully with the moral features of the scene. A foreigner in his prime, the only son of a widowed mother – cut down in his strength and murdered by a band of assassins in the streets of a great eastern capital, where all but the few members of the legations are still jealousy excluded – lay in the grave – round which the representatives of the greatest Powers in the West stood, mourning a wrong they were indeed helpless to redress.

Worse was to come the following year when, despite the placing of 150 guards round the British Legation, a band of fifteen desperadoes managed to penetrate right into its sleeping-quarters and seriously wounded two of its occupants. This incident delayed Alcock's return to Britain for leave until 1862. He published The Capital of the Tycoon *the following year. In one of its most widely-quoted passages he sketched out what was to prove an enduring characterization of Japan as 'topsy-turvy' land:*

Japan is essentially a country of paradoxes and anomalies, where all – even familiar things – put on new faces, and are curiously reversed. Except that they do not walk on their heads instead of their feet, there are few things in which they do not seem, by some occult law, to have been impelled in a perfectly opposite direction, and a reversed order. They write from top to bottom, from right to left, in perpendicular instead of horizontal lines; and their books begin where ours end, thus furnishing examples of the curious pefection this rule of contraries has attained. Their locks, though imitated from Europe, are all made to lock by turning the key from left to right. The course of all sublunary things appears reversed. Their day is for the most part our night; and this principle of antagonism crops out in the most unexpected bizarre way in all their moral being, customs and habits. I leave to philosophers the explanation – I only speak to the facts. There old men fly kites while the children look on; the carpenter uses his plane by drawing it *to* him, and their tailors stitch *from* them; they mount their horses from the off-side – the horses stand in the stables with their heads where we place their tails, and the bells to their harness are always on the hind quarters instead of the front; ladies black their teeth instead of keeping them white, and their anti-crinoline tendencies are carried to the point of seriously interfering not only with grace of movement but with all locomotion, so tightly are the lower limbs, from the waist downwards, girt round with their garments; – and finally, the utter confusion of sexes in the public bath-houses, making that correct, which we in the West deem so shocking and improper, I leave as I find it – a problem to solve.

If Sir Rutherford Alcock returned to Britain eager to inform his countrymen what The Capital of the Tycoon *was like, the Japanese were equally eager to find out what London was like. The 1862* Compendium of Famous Places in Barbarian Countries *described it thus:*

Yokohama – from fishing-village to modern port in half a century

There are a great many buildings, and the whole population is prosperous. The river is spanned by a large bridge 1800 feet long and 40 feet wide. There are three light towers which are lit at night for the benefit of travellers crossing the bridge. The bank of the river is dominated by an imposing fortress. In various parts of the city English goods are traded with merchants from all over the world. The mouth of the river is so choked with ships that one would believe one was on dry land. The population is large, and the number of students normally at university is never less than several tens of thousands. The women are extremely lustful and the men are both shrewd and cunning. To fulfil their ambitions they build large ships with which to sail the oceans of the world. They trade in all manner of goods and make enormous profits for themselves. They have 28,000 merchantmen with 185,000 officers on board. The monarch's ship has 40 cannons and there are eight hundred or more ships with 120 cannons each . . .

Lieutenant J.M.W. Silver of the Royal Marines served as a member of the British garrison in Japan in 1864–5 and in 1867 published a brief, colour-illustrated account of his observations entitled Sketches of Japanese Manners and Customs. *Intended as an earnest of his 'humble efforts to assist in the elucidation of the social condition of a distant and comparaitvely unknown race', Lt. Silver's book carries no pretensions to scholarly status nor claims to be a systematic survey. Indeed, the chapter-headings reveal no discernibly logical sequence, starting with 'Festivals and Holidays' and ending with 'Love of Flowers' and affording equal attention to 'The Court of the Mikado' on the one hand and 'Fires and Fire Brigades' on the other. Stevens clearly wrote about what he regarded as curious, surprising or shocking but, if some of his judgments are naive or prudish, his spelling eccentric and his apprehensions occasionally erroneous, he also reveals himself as warm-hearted in his willingness to praise or applaud.*

The following selection of passages relate to aspects of Japanese life of which the author evidently had some first-hand experience:

Fires and Fire Brigades

Fires are necessarily frequent, as the majority of the houses are constructed of wood; and such dangerous articles as paper-lanterns, small charcoal fireboxes, and movable open stoves, for household purposes, are in common use. The candles burnt in the paper-lanterns render them extremely dangerous, as they are fixed by a socket inside the lower end of the candle, which fits on a peg in the lantern – generally very loosely; and as they flare a great deal, very little wind or motion will cause a conflagration.

Fires are mostly attributed, however, to the 'chebache' (*hibachi*) or small charcoal fire-box, which is used for smoking purposes. It is placed on a small stand in the middle of the thickly-matted rooms, the smokers sitting round drinking *saki*, and occasionally filling their small pipes. Their method of smoking, like all the rest of their habits, is remarkably peculiar; for, after inhaling a few whiffs, the smoker invariably knocks out the half-consumed remnant on the 'chebache', and, presently refilling, commences another pipe, and so on, two or three times in succession, rarely troubling himself about the ashes of the last, which the slightest current of air may carry unperceived to smoulder in the combustible flooring.

Fires occur frequently, notwithstanding the great precautions which are taken for their prevention. Town and country are divided into districts, for which certain of the inhabitants are responsible. Each of these has its alarm, with observatory and regular watchers; while every guard-house is provided with a supply of ladders, buckets and other necessary implements. Whenever a gale is coming on, the . . . 'watch and fire look-outs', who on

Kenjutsu

ordinary occasions only go their rounds by night, parade the town with rattles and clanking iron instruments, as a warning to the people to keep their fires low.

They have numerous fire-brigades which are well-organized and remarkably efficient . . . The engines in present use are made of wood, and, though simple, are efficient in damping the roofs of houses . . . putting out embers, and playing upon the firemen . . . The Japanese, however, are thoroughly aware of the superiority of our engines, which will probably soon take the place of their own, as the people are singularly quick in availing themselves of anything useful.

The townspeople generally calculate on being burnt out once in every seven years, and whenever this calamity falls upon them, no time is lost in rebuilding. For instance, in December, 1864, a fragment of blazing wood, from a fire which destroyed the United Service Club at Yokohama, was blown across to the village of Omura . . . which was half burnt down, greatly endangering the General Small-pox Hospital and the huts of the Royal Marine Battalion in its rear. But early next morning, while the embers of the old houses were still smoking, new ones were in course of erection, and before night some of the industrious occupants were fairly roofed in afresh.

A Military Review

A review given by the two ministers for foreign affairs to Sir Rutherford Alcock, shortly before his departure, was a very imposing spectacle. The approach of the ministers was announced by the beating of drums . . . and the blowing of conch-shells, each instrument being sounded three times in succession, at short intervals. Men in armour carrying banners, bearing the Tycoon's crest, headed the procession. They were followed by a large drum in a square case, carried by two men, and the conch-blowers; then came a number of spear-men in armour; officers on horseback immediately preceding the ministers. On arriving at the ground they dismounted, and were received by Sir Rutherford Alcock, the remainder of their retinue passing on and forming in rear of the others, to the left of the English garrison, consisting of the second battalion of the 20th Regiment, the Royal Marine battalion, and detachments of Royal Artillery, of the 67th Regiment, and Beloochees (Baluchis), who were drawn up in brigade in honour of the occasion. At the request of the ministers the garrison marched past and performed a few manoeuvres, concluding with discharging blank cartridge in squares and in skirmishing order. The rapidity of the fire appeared to make a great impression on them. This over, the Japanese performance commenced; which was a representation of their ancient order of battle, the retainers dividing and forming in lines opposite one another, and about one hundred yards apart.

The proceedings were conducted by two marshals on foot; they began by forming the spear-men in line, with emphatic guttural commands, stamping of the feet, and flourishing of gilt batons, to the end of which wisps of paper were attached. All were habited in magnificent armour: some wore complete suits of mail; others chain armour, lined with gorgeous silks. Broad lacquered hats were here and there substituted for helmets; or both were dispensed with, and the temples of the combatants bound with linen cloth, which is their usual head-dress in action. Presently a signal was given, on which the opposing lines commenced simultaneously to 'mark line double'. At a second signal they faced into Indian file, and the marshals, placing themselves at their head, led them off at a swinging trot, the whole party flinging up their heels like boys playing at 'follow my leader', until startling guttural shouts from the marshals caused the glittering lines to halt and face each other. The horsemen, who had hitherto taken no part in the pageant, were now stationed in rear of the centre of the respective lines, and added greatly to the effect by their crested helmets, their richly gilt armour, and the heraldic banners, which were attached to the back of the cuirass and floated about two feet over their heads. As soon as the horsemen were stationed the exciting part of the sham-fight began, by the lines being wheeled backwards and forwards in wings from the centre, and into zigzag formations from central points, with a slow 'stamp-and-go' march, the spears being flourished with each motion and pointed high and low, and right and left, as in our bayonet exercise. The marshals regulated the movements of their respective lines with great accuracy, the one being retired directly the other advanced, so that the relative distance was never altered. After a time both parties suddenly assumed a sitting posture and exchanged howls of defiance, which grew fiercer and fiercer, until a simultaneous rush, as if to engage, finished the performance, from which the representatives of barbaric warfare retired amid the hearty cheers of the representatives of the bayonet and rifle.

Sumo Wrestling

Their principal athletic amusement is wrestling, which may be regarded as the national game of the country. It is very generally practised, and pairs of 'brawny fellows' are to be frequently met with of an evening in the outskirts of towns and villages, either crouched down in the preliminary attitude, which resembled that of angry fighting-cocks, or dragging one another to and fro like frogs struggling over a choice morsel. The game is necessarily a dragging and pulling one, its grand object being to force the opponent beyond a certain boundary.

So popular is it, that in addition to public performers, who travel about the country exhibiting their prowess, the *Daimios* (nobles) keep private bands: each district has some especial champion; and every Japanese a favourite 'smoo', as they term the wrestlers, whose exploits are canvassed with an enthusiasm totally at variance with the stolid indifference which usually characterises the people, when any subject is broached that does not directly concern their ordinary vocations.

The professional wrestlers are generally men of Herculean proportions. From constant practice they attain a muscular development that would eclipse that of our prize-ring champions; but their paunchy figures and sluggish movements render any further comparison impossible, as they neither practise nor appreciate what we call training. Size and weight are prized more than activity in the limited arena to which their performances are confined: so, instead of walking down superabundant flesh, they endeavour to increase it. . . .

. . . the Great Wrestling Amphitheatre at Yeddo conveys a fair idea of the estimation in which athletic games are held by the Japanese. The enclosure is capable of holding several thousand spectators, and is always filled when a match of importance takes place.

In the centre is the 'docho' (*dojo*) or 'boundary ring', which is about eighteen feet in diameter. The game is generally decided by one or other of the combatants being forced against this boundary; for, although a fair throw counts, it rarely decides the mastery, as the great weight and the crouching position of the wrestlers necessitate dragging, pushing and even carrying; and the tenacity of their grasp is such, that any other results are almost impossible.

The price of admission to these exhibitions is very low; and, like everything else of a public nature, is regulated by the government. Officials are appointed to superintend the arrangements, and to see that no accidents arise from overcrowding.

Before each wrestling-match commences, the . . . judge who superintends it, shouts out the names and exploits of

the contenders, who, after kowtowing very ceremoniously to one another, rise to the preliminary attitude.

At a signal from the judge the combatants commence. At first they move cautiously about the centre of the ring, watching a favourable opportunity to close, which they presently do with deep guttural exclamations. Then great working of muscle and tugging and straining follow, the spectators cheering on their respective favourites, until the fall of the judge's fan . . . proclaims the victor.

Thundering plaudits greet the hero of the occasion, who presently strolls about among the assembled multitude, attended by his . . . servant who collects the offerings with which they liberally reward his exertions. When money fails, articles of clothing are frequently bestowed – and sometimes too freely, as it is by no means unusual for both sexes to half denude themselves at these exhibitions; and it is a favourite joke with the women to send their male friends to redeem the articles from the wrestler.

An Execution

Crimes against property are rare in Japan, which is owing to the high-spirited and honourable feelings that actuate all classes of the community; but from the feudal nature of the government, the small value attached to life, and the deadly weapons constantly carried by the military classes, who are notoriously proud and revengeful, crimes against the person are very frequent.

A great check upon criminal offences is the severity of the punishments inflicted, and the disgrace entailed upon the culprit's family. Although the laws are extremely severe, and in their administration there is neither jury nor counsel, justice is delivered with great impartiality; and the judge, who is generally the governor of the town or district in which the offence has been committed, is entrusted with considerable discretionary power.

. . . public exposure is associated with all Japanese punishments, and is said to be in itself a great preventive of crime, as the spirited Japanese dread being held up to the reprobation of their acquaintance more than they fear the extreme penalty of the law.

. . . The culprit is bound on a horse, and is preceded by a placard, borne by his relatives or neighbours, and indicating his crime. In this manner he is conducted through the town to the place of execution, where his sentence is read to him. He is then placed (with his limbs still bound) over a freshly-dug hole where he is supported by his relatives till the executioner's sword performs its task.

After execution, the heads of malefactors are generally exposed: that of Simono Sedgi the lonin [*ronin meaning masterless samurai*], who was decapitated in the presence of the British garrison of Yokohama, for being the organizer of the assassination of Major Baldwin and Lieutenant Bird of Her Majesty's 20th Regiment, was exhibited on the public stand at the guard-house at the entrance of the town.

This man was a fair specimen of the lonin type, and was a most determined ruffian, whose whole life had been a career of crime.

When exposed in the streets of Yokohama the day preceding his execution, he conducted himself with great bravado, remarking on the improvements in the town since he last visited it, and expressing his regret that he had not killed a consul.

At the place of execution he made an impassioned speech, in which he declared that he was a gentleman by birth, and had studied the arts and sciences, and never believed the government would sacrifice a Japanese for the death of a foreigner. He said that the days would come when they would repent the encouragement they were now giving to strangers; and ended by complimenting the executioner on his well-known skill.

Spies and Baths

There are two Japanese customs so diametrically opposed to English ideas, and so materially affecting the national character, that it is necessary to call special attention to them.

The espionage system is perhaps the strangest, as every one in the country is subjected to it, from the Mikado and Tycoon, or spiritual and temporal emperors, to the humblest of the people.

All offices of importance are double; that is to say, every governor of a town or district is associated with a vice-governor, who . . . is in turn spied upon by others. In this way a constant check is kept upon the executive of the empire.

In addition to this acknowledged system, government officials are frequently watched by secret spies, who, for aught they know, may be some apparently trusted friend: so that, even in the absence of their double, they can never be certain that they are free from supervision.

In private life families spy on each other, for which purpose they are divided into coteries of five households, the heads of which are not only responsible for them-

Silk export became the major foreign currency earner

selves, their families and servants, but also for the other members of the coterie; and any wrong-doing in one household must be immediately reported to the proper authorities, to secure the rest from sharing in the punishment of the offence.

To such an extent is this system of responsibility carried, that a whole district sometimes suffers for the offence of one of its residents . . . This constant espionage has, of course, a very pernicious effect upon the character of the people, as it necessarily instils feelings of distrust and suspicion among near neighbours. Yet it is marvellous how well their social system works . . .

The other notable peculiarity is the indiscriminate manner in which the sexes mingle in the public bath-houses . . . There men, women and children perform their ablutions together, with all the apparent innocency of our first parents. The proceedings are conducted with perfect order and good-nature. The steaming occupants make way for one another with ball-room politeness; they laugh and chat over their tubs, discuss the public notices on the walls, or, maybe, saunter occasionally to the open door or window, to look at something which has attracted their attention, or to exchange greetings with a passing friend. All this is done with a freedom that speaks for itself of their utter unconsciousness of any impropriety in their conduct.

Frequently a lady is assisted by her husband in the cleansing process; and this is not necessarily a matrimonial compliment, as regular bathing-men are employed for the convenience of those who require such attention.

The *modus operandi* is very simple. The bather, after duly depositing his straw shoes at the door and paying a few cash for admittance, at once proceeds to disrobe himself, placing his garments in an allotted compartment. He then secures a tub, which is filled with lukewarm water, and, squatting down before it, lathers himself with a vegetable, soapy material, which is sewn up in a small bag. At this stage of the proceeding he will probably enter into conversation with his neighbours, complacently rejoicing in his soapiness until the remonstrances of the bathing-house man, or of some would-be possessor of his tub, compel him to finish his ablutions.

It would seem natural to conclude that such a system must have immoral effects, but the Japanese attribute no evil consequences to it. They say that, being accustomed to it from childhood, it only enables them to carry out those habits of cleanliness which distinguish alike their persons and their homes.

One of the fellow British residents that Lt. Silver would certainly have known would have been William Willis, the Legation doctor. A hulking 6ft 3in and 17 stones, the burly Ulsterman would have been difficult to miss. (We also know that both men were present at the execution described by Silver above.) Willis's fifteen years in Japan brought not only involvement in some of the most violent events which attended the downfall of the shogun's regime but also enabled him to make a crucial contribution to the introduction and advancement of western medicine and medical education in Japan.

Within days of moving into the Tozenji compound Willis was directly involved in a murderous night attack which marked the anniversary of the previous year's assault, an event which provoked in him some very John Bull reflections:

We live in a time when political changes of a stirring kind may be fairly anticipated . . . I fear the sword must cut the intricate knots in the long run. If Japan cannot learn to respect, she must be taught to fear . . . Japan is too much like China; a series of barbarities will ensue only to be repressed by a demonstration of power which will convince them that their very existence as a nation is at the mercy of the great powers of the West . . . The Japanese are proud and think, I imagine, that they are a match for any combination that may be brought against them. What

is the most horrible feature in the Japanese is their prone-
ness to assassinate in revenge and the daring and contempt
of life they display in carrying out their wicked designs.
No man here but must look upon his revolver as his
greatest friend . . . It is a state of society which cannot
always last . . . that day will come . . . when an
Englishman's blood will be the most precious thing in the
country, but at present I fear it is held cheaply.

*These predictions proved to be remarkably accurate. Three
months later Willis was involved in an even more notorious
incident. A party of British riders, led by a Shanghai merchant,
Charles Richardson, blundered into the retinue of the ruler of
Satsuma.*
*The three men were cut down – Richardson fatally – the woman
fleeing to tell the dreadful tale. An impromptu posse of British
residents rode to the scene, the fearless Willis among the foremost:*

. . . about four miles on the Edo side of Kanagawa we,
after difficulty and being denied by the inhabitants,
discovered poor Richardson lying on the road side under a
sort of shed of mats fearfully cut up and quite dead. We
brought his body back to Yokohama where it was interred
next day with great solemnity. . . . We are, of course, all
anxiety to know how the Government will deal with these
outrages. I fear it will lead to nothing. It is so difficult for
the Government to get at the facts, but I imagine Japan is
like China, nothing without war. We are on smouldering
ashes here . . .

*Despite his anger Willis realized that there were faults on both
sides:*

The English . . . are more hated than any other foreigners
and I believe require to be more on the alert. It is easy
enough, I think, to understand why we are specially
disliked. We are not over considerate in regard to the
feelings or prejudices of foreigners. We have all the air, if
not insolence, of a dominant race; the facility with which
we use our hands and feet in support of an argument may
elicit respect but not esteem. We hold Eastern dignitaries
very cheap . . . We bully and beat the lower orders, and
respect in no way the higher classes . . . though some
Japanese may like you individually they hate your country
. . . We may disguise it as we like, we are a set of tyrants
from the moment we set foot on Eastern soil . . .

*Having failed to extract satisfaction from the Japanese authorities
over the 'Richardson incident' the British determined to send a
naval force against Kagoshima, capital of Satsuma, in distant
Kyushu. A final essay at diplomacy proving useless, bombard-
ment followed, with Willis among the eye-witnesses:*

There is no doubt Jack Tar is a fine fellow and England is
proud with good reason of her sailors for they fight with a
will . . . Our ship went in fourth, the flagship leading. It
was certainly a grand sight to see the *Euryalus* open fire and
watch the effect of the shots she was giving and getting in
splendid style, and the Japanese manned their guns like
brave men . . . It was really tremendous, every now and
then some lucky shot struck a gun turning it over and
effectually stopping its voice . . . We remain all night at
secure distance and watch the dreadful conflagration off
the shore, a great city in flames . . . It kept one spell-
bound . . .

*When he eventually learned how these events were received in
Britain Willis was incensed:*

I see there has been lots of talk about Japan. I can only say
the speakers for the most part knew but little of their
subject. We don't know much certainly out here about
Japan but we know more plainly than they do at home. To
talk about exports as amounting to only £14,000 when last

year they were nearly seven millions is very absurd. What does not appear to be duly appreciated at home is the importance of Japan; it is to the continent of Asia quite as important as England is to Europe. What is fatal to us here is the generally believed unimportance of Japan. We are drifting into war . . . Our Treaty Rights are mere waste paper . . . The conflagration once set up will extend like wild fire . . . However, we must go through with it and it will repay in the long run for Japan is a splendid country and the Japanese are a clever, intelligent race.

Willis's professional concerns were hardly less lurid than the violent events he was caught up in. He records dealing with cholera, malaria, smallpox, stab wounds, rabies and venereal disease; this last was so serious a problem among the British garrison and officials that he prepared a lengthy memorandum on the subject at the request of the Foreign Office.

In September 1866 Willis reluctantly accompanied Alcock's firebrand successor, Sir Harry Parkes, on a conciliatory visit to Kagoshima:

. . . I look upon our visit to Satsuma as a great piece of humbug and scarcely decent to sit down at meals with an old scoundrel who ordered poor Richardson's death . . . I am at least in a position to say that a more villainous expression of countenance I never saw and, were I the British Minister, I certainly would not have partaken of hospitality coming from such a quarter. We had a nauseatingly long dinner of fish and slush in which it floated . . . For my own part, I feel contaminated by contact with a murderer on convivial terms . . . I was glad when I turned my back on Kagoshima. I must, however, say it is one of the most glorious places of scenery . . .

When civil war did finally break out Satsuma was one of the leading clans fighting to 'restore' power to the puppet Emperor by overthrowing the rule of the Shoguns. British policy discreetly favoured the rebel side and thus, ironically, Willis found himself in a very different relationship with the men of Satsuma, as he explained to his chief:

I have the honour to report my return today, after an absence of a fortnight in surgical attendance, as directed by you, upon the men of the Satsuma Clan who were wounded in the recent fight between them and the Tycoon's forces in the neighbourhood . . .

I found on my arrival . . . over a hundred wounded men. Their injuries were almost exclusively the result of firearms. I notice this as it would seem to point to the comparatively little use that appears to have been made of the national weapon, the long two-handed sword . . . In twelve cases I found it necessary to perform amputation . . . I also performed a number of minor operations, such as extracting bullets, removing pieces of dead bone and opening abscesses. I administered chloroform to all my patients requiring the use of the knife, to the great satisfaction of the native doctors, and of the patients themselves . . . I devoted my time to teaching the Japanese doctors and hospital attendants the best methods known to me of treating wounds generally . . . I imparted such information as lay in my power upon all matter relating to gunshot injuries. I pointed out the necessity of splints and other mechanical appliances . . . and from the anxiety manifested to learn particulars on this subject, I am inclined to think the native doctors look forward to having their skill brought much into requisition. Before I left I caused, under my supervision . . . a native doctor to perform an amputation of the forearm . . .

I may perhaps here remark, as illustrating the state of transition through which this country is passing, that I found two systems of healing contending for mastery, one known as the Chinese and the other as the Dutch system. The latter . . . accepts European medicine as the standard for imitation. The professors of the Chinese system deny the advantage of operations, in place of which they employ complicated drugs and ointments, whilst the professors of the Dutch system advocate the use of the knife, which they lack the requisite skill to apply to good purpose . . .

Willis went on to treat hundreds more casualties on both sides during the civil war and then turned to establishing a teaching hospital – in Kagoshima.

It was to Algernon Bertram Mitford (1837–1916), later to become the first Baron Redesdale, that the English-speaking world owed its first eye-witness account of seppuku *– the practice of ritual disembowelment more vulgarly known as 'hara-kiri' (literally belly-slitting). Far from wishing to gratify a prurient curiosity Mitford wrote to present to the readers of the* Cornhill Magazine *a scrupulous and sensitive description which would engage their sympathy and enlarge their understanding.*

Few men were better suited to the task. Educated at Eton and Christ Church, Oxford, Mitford entered the Foreign Office at the age of twenty-one and was almost immediately despatched to China. He proved to be an able linguist and within a year of arriving in Japan in 1866 as Third Acting Secretary had acquired sufficient fluency to enable him to exercise a critical approach in getting to grips with his new surroundings.

Mitford's private letters reveal a marked lack of enchantment with his new posting. Describing Edo (Tokyo) to his father he pictures it unlovingly as:

. . . low narrow buildings in straight lines round dirty squares. I say dirty advisedly for although there is great cleanliness inside the houses the filthy stenches and abominations outside are as bad as China.

Other places were even worse:

There can be nothing more uninteresting than a Japanese town. There is neither colour nor architecture and Osaka is certainly almost exceptionally ugly, being entirely commercial and industrial.

In February 1868 at Hyogo (now the port of Kobe) a samurai commander ordered his men to open fire on a contingent of western troops in response to an alleged act of disrespect. Despite a brisk exchange of shots no one was killed on either side but the outraged western powers demanded retribution. The new imperial regime, committed to a novel 'pro-foreign' policy, decided to placate them by ordering the seppuku of the luckless samurai commander who had given the order to open fire. It was this event that Mitford was called upon to attend as one of seven official western witnesses.

On the morning immediately after the seppuku Mitford, on the orders of his chief, Sir Harry Parkes, drafted an account of what he had seen. This was then sent on to the Foreign Office as an addendum to routine despatches. Eighteen months later it was to serve Mitford as the basis for his Cornhill article.

In reading the passage one should note particularly both the author's consistent concern to convey a sense of the dignity of the occasion and his careful choice of language. Any suggestion of the 'barbaric' or 'picturesque' is eschewed. Where Mitford thought no appropriate English words existed Japanese terms are used.

The entire procedure is presented with the samurai in the role of 'gentleman' – the Japanese equivalent of a reader of the Cornhill Magazine.

Mitford begins with a definition, supposedly from a rare Japanese manuscript:

Seppuku is the mode of suicide, adopted by Samurai when they have no alternative but to die. Some there are, who having committed some crime which does not put them outside the pale of the privilege of the Samurai class, are ordered by their superiors to put an end to their own lives.

The ceremony took place at 10.30 at night in the main hall of a temple:

Crowded living conditions made neighbourliness an essential virtue

It was an imposing scene. A large hall with a high roof supported by dark pillars of wood. From the ceiling hung a profusion of those huge gilt lamps and ornaments peculiar to Buddhist temples. In front of the altar, where the floor covered with beautiful white mats is raised some three or four inches from the ground, was laid a rug of scarlet felt. Tall candles placed at regular intervals gave out a mysterious light.

After an interval of a few minutes of anxious suspense Taki Zenzaburo, a stalwart man, thirty-two years of age, with a noble air, walked into the hall attired in his dress of ceremony, with the peculiar hempen cloth wings which are worn on great occasions . . . He was accompanied by a *kaishaku* and three officers who wore the jimbaori or war surcoat with gold tissue facings.

Mitford emphasised that his use of the unfamiliar word kaishaku *was deliberate because it was:*

. . . one to which our word 'executioner' is no equivalent term. The office is that of a gentleman . . . In this instance the *kaishaku* was a pupil of Taki Zenzaburo, and was selected by the friends of the latter from among their own number for his skill in swordsmanship.

Having bowed to the assembled company:

Slowly and with great dignity the condemned man mounted on to the raised floor, prostrated himself before the high altar twice and seated himself (that is in the Japanese fashion, his knees and toes touching the ground, and his body resting on his heels). In this position, which is one of respect, he remained until his death.

He was then given a razor-sharp, 9½-in wakizashi or dirk, which he took with both hands, raised respectfully to his head and then placed before him.

After another profound obeisance Zenzaburo, in a voice which betrayed just so much emotion and hesitation as might be expected from a man who is making a painful confession but with no sign of either in his face or manner spoke as follows: 'I and I alone unwarrantably gave the order to fire on the foreigners at Kobe and again as they tried to escape. For this crime I disembowel myself and I beg you who are present to do me the honour of witnessing the act . . .'

Bowing once more, the speaker allowed his upper garments to slip down to his girdle and remained naked to the waist. Carefully, according to custom, he tucked his sleeves under his knees to prevent himself falling backward; for a noble Japanese gentleman should die falling forwards. Deliberately, with a steady hand, he took the dirk that lay before him; he looked at it wistfully, almost affectionately; for a moment he seemed to collect his thoughts for the last time, and then stabbing himself deeply below the waist on the left hand side, he drew the dirk slowly to the right side, and, turning it in the wound, gave a slight cut upwards. During this sickeningly painful operation he never moved a muscle of his face. When he drew out the dirk, he leaned forward and stretched out his neck; an expression of pain for the first time crossed his face, but he uttered no sound. At that moment, the *kaishaku*, who, still crouching by his side, had been keenly watching his every movement, sprang to his feet, poised his sword for a second in the air; there was a flash, a heavy, ugly thud, a crashing fall; with one blow the head had been severed from the body.

A dead silence followed broken only by the hideous noise of the blood throbbing out of the inert heap before us, which but a moment before had been a brave and chivalrous man. It was horrible.

But it was also admirable:

The ceremony, to which the place and hour gave an additional solemnity, was characterised throughout by that extreme dignity and punctiliousness which are the distinctive marks of the proceedings of gentlemen of rank . . . While profoundly impressed by the terrible scene it was impossible at the same time not to be filled with admiration of the firm and manly bearing of the sufferer, and of the nerve with which the *kaishaku* performed his last duty to his master.

Mitford contributed two other articles to the Cornhill. *These were essentially translations of the sermons of a popular preacher,*

'What has most impressed me is the seeming joyousness of popular faith. I have seen nothing grim, austere or self-repressive. I have not even noted anything approaching the solemn . . . The people take their religion lightly and cheerfully . . . Blessed are they who do not too much fear the gods which they have made!'

Lafcadio Hearn, 1894

The arrangements of a Japanese theatre are simple enough, though rather peculiar. The centre is occupied by a pit divided into a number of little partitions about a yard square, reminding one of . . . a cabinet for bird's eggs . . . In each partition nests a Japanese family . . . The main action, of course, takes place on the front or principal stage, though the side stages are used both for action and for entry and exit. These facilities for entry from the back of the spectators are first-rate for surprises. While the audience is intent on the tragic event that thrills the stage, a ghost or demon glides in from behind, unobserved perhaps until it reaches the front . . . In a wicker cage on the left of the front stage, kept pretty well out of sight, are the orchestra. It is a pity that they can't be kept out of hearing also, for of all the caterwauling. . . .'

Douglas Sladen, 1908

his concern being to show that the Japanese, although not Christian, did indeed possess a high moral code and could not be dismissed as savages. In 1872 Mitford published a substantial volume, Tales of Old Japan, *which reprinted his account of the* seppuku *along with a number of heroic samurai stories, including the saga of 'The Forty-Seven Ronin', which is to the Japanese what Robin Hood is to the English – except that it happens to be entirely true.*

After an interval of almost forty years Mitford returned to Japan in 1906, accompanying Prince Arthur of Connaught on his mission to invest the Emperor of Japan with the Order of the Garter.

W.E. Griffis' relationship with Japan lasted for more than half a century. He was one of the very few who could claim to have experienced 'feudalism' at first hand, serving as a teacher in a remote province before Japan adopted centralized modernization as its national policy. He subsequently acted as an adviser on educational policy before returning to the United States to write what, for almost forty years, became the 'standard' American work on Japan – plus seventeen other books on the country, as well as hundreds of articles for newspapers, encyclopaedias and leading periodicals like Harper's, Scribner's *and the* North American Review. *Maintaining contact with a network of former students, who included future prime ministers, foreign ministers and ambassadors, Griffis came to be widely regarded as one of his country's leading experts on Japan. Although his actual period of residence lasted less than four years Griffis was an assiduous and skilful self-publicist, encouraged in his self-advancement by the belief that his career was guided by a higher power:*

Providence so ordered that I should see, when almost a baby, the launching, in 1850, of Commodore Perry's flagship, the frigate *Susquehanna*; that I should have as a classmate the son of our American Minister, Pruyn, who

had been in Japan; that I should during my four years at Rutgers College . . . teach the first Japanese students in America; that I should spend another four years in educational work in the interior and capital of Dai Nippon; that my sister Margaret Clark Griffis, should be the principal of the first government school for girls; and that I should remain on constant terms of intimacy with Nippon's sons and daughters ever since . . .

Griffis' original motives for going to Japan were a mixture of the idealistic and the worldly:

I can study and be ordained there, and God willing, return to my native land only one year later than if I staid [sic]. Beside the grand opportunities and culture, travel and good climate, and being under the special protection of the prince of the province, I can not only study on my theology, but collect materials to write a book. I can support my family at home, at least, pay the rent, and carpet the floors, and send handsome sums home, too.

Griffis' first sight of Fukui, capital of Echizen province, brought him back to earth with a bump:

. . . expecting at last to emerge into some splendid avenue . . . the scales fell from my eyes . . . I was amazed at the utter poverty of the people, the contemptible houses, and the tumble-down look of the city, as compared with the trim dwellings of an American town . . . I realized what a Japanese – an Asiatic city – was . . . I was disgusted.

But Griffis still set himself bold aims, which he confided in a letter to his sister:

. . . to make Fukuwi College the best in Japan, and to make a national textbook on Chemistry, to advocate the education of women, to abolish the drinking of *sake*, the

Tattooing

wearing of swords, the promiscuous bathing of the sexes . . . I want the Prince to feel that I am more than a time-serving foreigner.

Griffis was generously paid and treated with respect and kindness, the Echizen authorities acting as much like thoughtful hosts as employers, but he soon reached a shrewd understanding of the realization of his situation and wrote a warning article for Scientific American:

. . . this country is already overstocked with foreigners out of employment. I should advise no American to come to Japan, unless he has a position secured before he comes.

In regard to men appointed to offices with high sounding names and large salaries, I am afraid many people will be disappointed concerning Japan. The Japanese simply want helpers and advisers. They propose to keep the 'bossing', officering, and all the power in their own hands . . . All this 'taking charge of', 'being at the head of', 'organizing' etc., is sheer daydreaming . . . Nearly every appointee comes here 'to revolutionize' his department, but the Japanese don't want that. They want the foreigners to get into the traces, and pull just so fast as, and no faster than, their mighty enterprises can bear. Let it not be forgotten that this is an emphatically poor country now, and that millions of its people are very ignorant, and that it has just emerged from feudalism; and that therefore the rulers of Japan must go slowly and cautiously. Above everything else, it is not wise to put their soil or their enterprises too much into foreign hands, and to prove that Japanese nature is human nature, they like to do it themselves . . . Therefore, if a man means real hard work . . . and is willing to help without 'taking charge' of everything, let him try Japan. If he expects that the Japanese people wish to make him a Secretary of State, or Minister of Education, or Postmaster General, etc., he had better stay at home, because the Japanese people like to be officers themselves, and are neither children nor weak-minded.

Griffis worked himself hard and thought his students well worth the effort:

Here were nearly a thousand young samurai. What was one teacher among so many? Could it be possible that these could be trained and disciplined students? . . . A few months later and I had won their confidence and love. I found they were quite able to instruct me in many things . . . In pride and dignity of character, in diligence, courage, gentlemanly conduct, refinement and affection, truth and honesty, good morals, in so far as I knew or could see, they were my peers.

The Geisha

By filling every moment with purposeful activity Griffis kept homesickness at bay. His typical daily routine was as follows:

7 a.m. Rise and make toilet (bathing twice per week and shaving three times per week) followed by breakfast.

7.30 – 8 a.m. Reading Greek and devotion.

8 – 10 a.m. Study (usually Japanese, Physics or Chemistry).

10 – 12 Noon Teaching.

12 – 1 p.m. Lunch and Reading. 1 – 3 p.m. Teaching.

3 – 6 p.m. Walk.

6 – 6.30 p.m. Supper.

6.30 – 8 p.m. Japanese.

8 – 11 p.m. Writing.

That he saw worse perils than occasional loneliness is evident from a letter written to his sister about six months after his arrival in Fukui:

The young girl . . . whom I took for a servant to wait specifically on me proved to be very faithful, diligent and pleasant in every way, anticipated my every want, and made my house almost as comfortable as a home; I liked her very much. All of which to a sometimes weary and home-sick young man must necessarily be a strong temptation in his lonely hours. I found after two weeks, that she made too much comfort for me, and was too attractive herself . . . I sent her away, before temptation turned into sin . . . and now, though with less comfort and a more lonely house, I can let all my inner life be known to you without shame.

Griffis' first Christmas in Japan gave him a chance to return some of the hospitality that had been showered upon him:

I had unlimited quantities of chocolate and coffee made, a large box of soda biscuit, plenty of Japanese cake etc. Most of them had never before tasted either drink, so they tried both, and I kept their cups full . . . The American flag . . . was out in full glory and attracted much attention. Several strangers dropped in to see what was going on and they were also seized, dragged in, coffeed, caked and Happy Christmased . . . Of course, they inquired what the observance was for, and probably it was a new idea for many to know that any good thing came out of the Yasou (Jesus).

Griffis left Fukui after less than a year, having successfully angled for a job in the capital, which he found much altered in his brief absence:

Tokio is so modernized that I scarcely recognize it. No beggars, no guard-houses, no sentinels . . . no swords worn . . . new decencies and proprieties observed . . . more clothes. The age of pantaloon has come. . . . carriages numerous . . . Shops full of foreign wares and notions. Soldiers all uniformed . . . New bridges span the canals. Police in uniform . . . Railway nearly finished . . . Gold and silver coin in circulation . . . An air of bustle, energy and activity . . . Old Yedo has passed away forever. Tokio, the national capital is a cosmopolis.

In Tokyo Griffis taught not only science, but also geography, physiology, literature and even law; at the same time he continued to write articles, compile textbooks and guide-books and preach at the new Union Church of Yokohama.

It is perhaps ironic that, having warned his countrymen of the Japanese determination to uphold their own authority, Griffis should fall out with officialdom and have his contract terminated. He wrote home ruefully:

I am a little sorry, as I should like to have remained six months longer at least. After near three years service in a foreign land, I have in bank now, just enough to take me

home. For the future, however, I have no sort of fear, and though I never expect, nor care to be a rich man, not making wealth an object, I expect to win a name and place in my native land.

Griffis' magnum opus – The Mikado's Empire – *was published within two years of his return and went through no less than twelve editions between then and 1913. It was in many respects a sympathetic portrait and often keenly critical of western policy:*

There is no blacker page in history than the exactions and cruelties practised against Japan by the diplomatic representatives of the nations called Christian – in the sense of

their having the heaviest artillery. In their financial and warlike operations in Japan, the foreign ministers seem to have acted as if there was no day of judgement.

But Griffis did not seek to flatter Japan and was, for example, content to quote the anonymous dictum that:

The actual government of Japan is despotism tempered by assassination.

Griffis' summary of Japanese national character was complimentary but not uncritical:

In moral character the average Japanese is frank, honest, faithful, kind, gentle, courteous, confiding, affectionate, filial, loyal. Love of truth for its own sake, chastity, temperance are not characteristic virtues.

In 1891 the Japanese scholar Nitobe Inazo hailed Griffis' book as:

By far the best American work on Japan . . . no author has done more to present in attractive style the salient features of our tradition, history, manners and customs.

In 1908 the Japanese government recognized Griffis' achievement by honouring him with the Order of the Rising Sun, Fourth Class. Shortly before his death in 1928 it again honoured him by sponsoring a lengthy official visit, which included a triumphant return to Fukui, where the whole town turned out to greet him.

As a Japanese journalist graciously put it:

Had he no other claim to brilliance than his *The Mikado's Empire*, that alone would entitle him to front rank, for, in it Dr. Griffis saw in Japan, long before she had become one of the great powers of the world, the making of a great nation.

W.E. Griffis once noted that in Japan:

. . . the biography of a good woman is written in one word – obedience.

But, having summarized the matter with admirable conciseness, he also mused that:

The whole question of the position of Japanese women – in history, social life, education, employments, authorship, art, marriage, concubinage, prostitution, benevolent labor, the ideals of literature, popular superstitions etc., – discloses such a wide and fascinating field of inquiry that I wonder no one has as yet entered it.

Somebody had. By the time she read Griffis' words a fellow American, Alice Mabel Bacon, was already more than half way through the composition of Japanese Girls and Women. *As she freely acknowledged in her Preface, Alice Bacon was greatly*

'More precious in a woman is a virtuous heart than
a face of beauty.'
The Greater Learning for Women

assisted in the completion of her task by Griffis' own comments and, even more, by those of:

Miss Ume Tsuda, teacher of English in the Peeresses' School in Tokyo and an old and intimate friend.

As Miss Tsuda was, at the time of writing, on study-leave at exclusive Bryn Mawr College, as the book is dedicated to Countess Oyama, and as the author taught and socialized at the highest social level, it is clear that her book is written 'from the point of view of the refined and intelligent.' Despite this limitation of perspective the author was confident that she had something new to offer, a mode of encounter with Japan so far unknown to the West:

It seems necessary for a new author to give some excuse for her boldness in offering to the public another volume upon a subject already so well written up as Japan . . . While Japan as a whole has been closely studied . . . one half of the population has been left entirely unnoticed, passed over with brief mention, or altogether misunderstood. It is of this neglected half that I have written, in the hope that the whole fabric of Japanese social life will be better comprehended when the women of the country, and so the homes that they make, are better known and understood.

The reason why Japanese home-life is so little understood by foreigners, even by those who have lived long in Japan, is that the Japanese, under an appearance of frankness and candor, hides an impenetrable reserve in regard to all those personal concerns which he believes are not in the remotest degree the concerns of his foreign guest. Only life in the home itself can show what a Japanese home may be; and only by intimate association – such as no foreign man can ever hope to gain – with the Japanese ladies themselves can much be learned of the thoughts and daily lives of the best Japanese women.

The author takes as the framework for her book the normal life-cycle of a woman and the social hierarchy, from courtier to domestic servant. She begins with childhood:

After all these festivities, a quiet, undisturbed life begins for the baby, – a life which is neither unpleasant nor unhealthful. It is not jolted, rocked, or trotted to sleep; it is allowed to cry if it chooses, without anybody's supposing that the world will come to an end because of its crying; and its dress is loose and easily put on, so that very little time is spent in the tiresome process of dressing and undressing. Under these conditions the baby thrives and grows strong and fat; learns to take life with some philosophy, even at a very early age; and is not subject to fits of hysterical or passionate crying, brought on by much jolting or trotting, or by the wearisome process of pinning, buttoning, tying and strings and thrusting of arms into tight sleeves.

With the baby tied to her back, a woman is able to care for a child, and yet go on with her household labors, and baby watches over mother's or nurse's shoulder, between naps taken at all hours, the processes of drawing water, washing and cooking rice, and all the varied work of the house. Imperial babies are held in the arms of someone night and day, from the moment of birth until they have learned to walk, a custom which seems to render the lot of the high-born infant less comfortable in some ways than that of the plebeian child.

The flexibility of the knees, which is required for comfort in the Japanese method of sitting, is gained in very early youth by the habit of setting a baby down with its knees bent under it, instead of with its legs out straight before it, as seems to us the natural way.

As if to prove that her judgement of what is 'natural' is based on science and not prejudice the author then diverts her reader into a lengthy footnote:

That the position of the Japanese in sitting is really unnatural and unhygienic, is shown by recent measurements taken by the surgeons of the Japanese army. These measurements prove that the small stature of the Japanese is due largely to the shortness of the lower limbs, which are out of proportion to the rest of the body. The sitting from early childhood upon the legs bent at the knee, arrests the development of that part of the body, and produces an actual deformity in the whole nation. This deformity is less noticeable among the peasants, who stand and walk so much as to secure proper development of the legs; but among merchants, literary men, and others of sedentary habits, it is most plainly to be seen. The

introduction of chairs and tables, as a necessary adjunct of Japanese home life, would doubtless in time alter the physique of the Japanese as a people.

Returning to the theme of early learning the author notes that 'among the lower classes' babies, even a few weeks old, are taken to the bath-house:

To a baby's delicate skin, the first bath or two is usually a severe trial, but it soon becomes accustomed to a high temperature, and takes its bath, as it does everything else, placidly and in public.

Diet is another topic for investigation and reflection:

Born into a country where cow's milk is never used, the Japanese baby is wholly dependent upon its mother for milk, and is not weaned entirely until it reaches the age of three or four years, and is able to live upon the ordinary food of the class to which it belongs. There is no intermediate stage . . .

In consequence, partly, of the lack of proper nourishment after the child is too old to live wholly upon its mother's milk, and partly, perhaps, because of the poor food that the mothers, even of the higher classes, live upon, many babies in Japan are afflicted with disagreeable skin troubles, especially of the scalp and face . . . Another consequence, as I imagine, of the lack of proper food at the teething period, is the early loss of the child's first teeth, which usually turn black and decay some time before the second teeth begin to show themselves. With the exception of these two troubles, Japanese babies seem healthy, hearty, and happy to an extraordinary degree . . . One striking characteristic of the Japanese baby is, that at a very early age it learns to cling like a kitten to the back of whoever carries it, so that it is really difficult to drop it through carelessness, for the baby looks out for its own safety like a young monkey . . . and this clinging with arms and legs is, perhaps, a valuable part of the training which gives to the whole nation the peculiar quickness of motion and hardness of muscle that characterize them from childhood. It is the agility and muscular quality that belong to wild animals, that we see something of in the Indian, but to a more marked degree in the Japanese, especially of the lower classes.

The transition from crawling to walking, Miss Bacon argues, also has long-run implications for adult life:

The Japanese baby's first lessons in walking are taken under favorable circumstances. With feet comfortably shod in the soft *tabi*, or mitten-like sock, babies can tumble about as they like, with no bump or bruise, upon the soft matted floors of the dwelling houses. There is no furniture to fall against, and nothing about the room to render falling a thing to be feared. After learning the art of walking in the house, the baby's first attempts out of doors are hampered by the *zori* or *geta* – a light straw sandal or small wooden clog attached to the foot by a strap passing between the toes . . . This somewhat cumbersome and inconvenient footgear must cause many falls at first, but baby's experience in the art of balancing upon people's backs now aids in this new art of balancing upon the little wooden clogs . . . older children run, jump, hop on one foot, and play all manner of active games that would wrench our ankles and toes out of all possibility of usefulness. This foot gear, while producing an awkward, shuffling gait, has certain advantages over our own, especially for children whose feet are growing rapidly. The *geta*, even if outgrown, can never cramp the toes nor compress the ankles. If the foot is too long for the clog the heel laps over behind, but the toes do not suffer, and the use of the *geta* strengthens the ankles but affording no artificial aid or support, and giving to all the muscles of

foot and leg free play, with the foot in a natural position. The toes of the Japanese retain their prehensile qualities to a surprising degree, and are used, not only for grasping the foot gear, but among mechanics almost like two supplementary hands to aid in holding the thing worked upon. Each toe knows its work and does it, and they are not reduced to the dull uniformity that characterizes the toes of a leather-shod nation.

As in the realm of physical development so in the sphere of moral growth Miss Bacon, perhaps with an over-eager teacher's eye, sees early learning as the key:

As our little girl emerges from babyhood she finds the life opening before her a bright and happy one, but one hedged about closely by the proprieties, and one in which, from babyhood to old age, she must expect to be always under the control of one of the stronger sex. Her position will be an honourable and respected one only as she learns in her youth the lesson of cheerful obedience, of pleasing manners, and of personal cleanliness and neatness . . . There is no career or vocation open to her . . . and her greatest happiness is to be gained, not by cultivation of the intellect, but by the early acquisition of the self-control which is expected of all Japanese women to an even greater degree than of the men. This self-control must consist, not only in the concealment of all the outward signs of any disagreeable emotion, – whether of grief, anger or pain, – but in the assumption of a cheerful smile and agreeable manner under even the most distressing of circumstances. The duty of self-restraint is taught to the little girls of the family from the tenderest years; it is their great moral lesson, and is expatiated upon at all times by their elders . . . The effect of this teaching is seen in the attractive but dignified manners of the Japanese women, and even of the very little girls. They are not forward nor pushing, neither are they awkwardly bashful; there is no self-consciousness,

'For most Japanese girls their youth is a training for greater responsibilities'

Alice M. Bacon

'In everything she must avoid extravagance . . . and never give way to luxury and pride.'
The Greater Learning for Women

neither is there any lack of savoir faire; a childlike simpli-city is united with a womanly consideration for the comfort of those around them. A Japanese child seems to be the product of a more perfect civilization than our own, for its comes into the world with little of the savagery and barbarian bad manners that distinguish children in this country, and the first ten or fifteen years of its life do not seem to be passed in one long struggle to acquire a coating of good manners that will help to render it less obnoxious in polite society. How much of the politeness of the Japanese is the result of training, and how much is inherited from generations of civilized ancestors, it is difficult to tell . . .

Isabella Bird (1831–1904) was a sickly woman from a pious household, who was advised to travel for the sake of her health. Whether the diagnosis was faulty or the remedy was correct the results were spectacular. On her first trip, at the age of forty-one, she found the Antipodes too dull, so diverted to the Sandwich Islands, climbed a volcano in Hawaii, rode through the Rockies in winter and showed the good sense not to marry a drunken, poetry-loving rapscallion of a mountain-man who fell hopelessly in love with her. Returning to England, she was so shocked by a proposal of marriage from her family doctor that she set off for Japan. Miss Bird's account of her experiences is well titled Unbeaten Tracks in Japan *for she was anything but content to follow the well-worn path of the timorous tourist. The Preface explains her purpose in publication with brisk directness:*

. . . I decided to visit Japan, attracted less by the reputed excellence of its climate than by the certainty that it possessed, in an especial degree, those sources of novel and sustained interest which conduce so essentially to the enjoyment and restoration of a solitary health-seeker. The climate disappointed me, but, though I found the country a study rather than a rapture, its interest exceeded my largest expectations.

This is not a 'Book on Japan' but a narrative of travels in Japan . . . and it was not till I had travelled for some months in the interior of the main island and in Yezo (Hokkaido) that I decided that my materials were novel enough to render the contribution worth making. From Nikko northwards my route was altogether off the beaten track, and had never been traversed in its entirety by any European. I lived among the Japanese, and saw their mode of living, in regions unaffected by European contact. As a lady travelling alone, and the first European lady who had been seen in several districts through which my route lay, my experiences differed more or less widely from those of preceding travellers; and I am able to offer a fuller account of the aborigines of Yezo, obtained by actual acquaintance with them than has hitherto been given.

At first glance one might fear a sniffy shrillness in the author's forthright denunciations:

The Japanese are the most irreligious people that I have ever seen – their pilgrimages are picnics, and their religious festivals fairs.

Indeed, religion is a theme to warm her:

An Imperial throne founded on an exploded religious fiction, a State religion receiving an outward homage from those who ridicule it, scepticism rampant among the educated classes, and an ignorant priesthood lording it over the lower classes; an Empire with a splendid despot-ism for its apex, and naked coolies for its base, a bald materialism its highest creed and material good its goal, reforming, destroying, constructing, appropriating the fruits of Christian civilization, but rejecting the tree from which they spring – such are among the contrasts and incongruities everywhere!

The kago is used in the mountains as the equivalent of the rickshaw

Of the Geku shrine near Yamada this daughter of a scholarly clergyman wrote with indignation:

The impression produced by the whole resembles that made upon the minds of those who have made the deepest researches into Shinto – there is nothing, and all things, even the stately avenues of the Geku, lead to NOTHING.

Exasperation did not, however, prevent her from being a keen and perceptive observer, capable of formulating a shrewd cultural judgement from even such apparently trivial phenomena as Tokyo shop-signs:

Confectioners usually display a spiked white ball a foot and a half in diameter; sake-sellers a cluster of cypress trimmed into a sphere; the sellers of the crimson pigment with which women varnish their lips a red flag; goldbeaters a great pair of square spectacles, with gold instead of glass; druggists and herbalists a big bag resembling in shape the small ones used in making their infusions; kite-makers a cuttle fish; sellers of cut flowers a small willow tree; dealers in dried and salt fish, etc., two fish coloured red, and tied together by the gills with straw, indicating that they can supply the gifts which it is usual to make to betrothed persons; but the Brobdignagian signs in black, red and gold which light up the streets of Canton, are too 'loud' and explicit for Japanese taste, which prefers the simple and symbolical.

Most western writers about Japan seem to have lost all sense of restraint or proportion when it came to the subject of women. As they were almost all men this is perhaps not surprising. Miss Bird offers her own characteristically acerbic observation:

. . . as may be expected, suicide is more common among women than men . . . they usually go out at night, and

after filling their capacious hanging sleeves with stones, jump into a river or well.

Nor was Miss Bird apt to rhapsodize when describing places:

Yokohama does not improve on further acquaintance. It has a dead – alive look. It has irregularity without picturesqueness, and the grey sky, grey sea, grey houses and grey roofs look harmoniously dull.

No view of Tokiyo, leaving out the impression produced by size, is striking, indeed there is a monotony of meanness about it . . . As a city it lacks concentration. Masses of greenery, lined or patched with grey, and an absence of beginning or end, look suburban rather than metropolitan. Far away in the distance are other grey patches; you are told that those are still Tokiyo, and you ask no more. It is a city of 'magnificent distances' without magnificence.

A single look at Hakodate itself makes one feel that it is Japan all over. The streets are very wide and clean, but the houses are mean and low. The city looks as if it had just recovered from a conflagration. The houses are nothing but tinder . . . There is not an element of permanence in the wide and windy streets. It is an increasing and busy place; it lies for two miles along the shore, and has climbed the hill till it can go no higher; but still houses and people look poor.

Hakodate is the gateway to Hokkaido, annexed to Japan barely a decade before Miss Bird's arrival. Of this large and virtually unpopulated island she noted drily:

Yezo is to the main island of Japan what Tipperary is to an Englishman . . . Nobody comes here without meeting with something queer, and one or two tumbles.

And it is evident that her interest in the Ainu was prompted more by scientific curiosity that affection or respect:

An avenue of torii marks the entrance to a Shinto shrine

The 'hairy Ainos', as these savages have been called, are stupid, gentle, good-natured and submissive. They are a wholly distinct race from the Japanese. In complexion they resemble the people of Spain and Southern Italy, and the expression of the face and the manner showing courtesy are European rather than Asiatic. If not taller, they are of a much broader and heavier make than the Japanese; the hair is jet black, very soft, and on the scalp forms thick, pendant masses, occasionally wavy, but never showing any tendency to curl. The beard, moustache, and eyebrows are very thick and full, and there is frequently a heavy growth of stiff hair on the chest and limbs. The neck is short, the brow high, broad and massive, the nose broad and inclined to flatness, the mouth wide but well formed, the line of the eyes and and eyebrows perfectly straight, and the frontal sinuses well marked. Their language is a very simple one. They have no written characters, no literature, no history, very few traditions, and have left no impression on the land from which they have been driven.

Regarding the future prospects of the Ainu she was scarcely encouraging:

They are . . . completely irreclaimable as the wildest of nomad tribes, and contact with civilization, where it exists, only debases them. Several young Ainos were sent to Tokiyo, and educated and trained in various ways, but as soon as they returned to Yezo they relapsed into savagery, retaining nothing but a knowledge of Japanese. They are charming in many ways, but make one sad, too, by their stupidity, apathy, and hopelessness, and all the sadder that their numbers appear to be again increasing; and as their physique is very fine, there does not appear to be a prospect of the race dying out at present.

Isabella returned to England and married the good doctor after all. He knew her strengths – 'the appetite of a tiger and the digestion of an ostrich' – and her weakness – 'I have only one formidable rival in Isabella's affections, and that is the high tableland of Central Asia.' His sudden death five years later set Isabella on her travels again . . .

Throughout the 1980s Japan's attachment to whaling provoked international criticism. A century ago western observers were similarly horrified, as this description, written by the Revd R.B. Grinnan for the Japan Mail *testifies:*

The signals are a very important part of the work. Men with glasses are arranged on three different mountains, one above the other. The man from the highest point, being able to see furthest, gives the first notice as to the approach of a whale by lighting a fire and raising a smoke, and at the same time by means of his flag he signals to the men on the mountain below, and they in turn signal to the boats. It is necessary for the men in the boats to know beforehand what kind of whale is coming, also his size and distance from the land; for the attack differs according to these three things. The species of the whale is known in most cases by the manner in which the water is spouted up. The first thing to be done when the boats move out, is to put down the nets across the path of the whale. This is rather difficult to do correctly, for in the first place they must be arranged according to the species of the whale. Another thing to be calculated on is strength and course of the tide. One fighting boat goes to each net boat, to assist in arranging the nets in their proper order. Not all of the nets are put down at first . . . After the first net is laid, the others are all arranged a little to the right or left, so that when all the nets are down they slant off to one side or the other, and thus cover a broader space across the path of the whale. As soon as the nets are arranged the net boats draw off on each side and look on. Then some of the fighting boats go around behind the whale to attack from that

Ainu: 'Both sexes are of a mild and amiable disposition, but are terribly addicted to drunkenness.'
Basil Hall Chamberlain

point, while others arrange themselves on the sides so as to drive the whale into the nets. Those from behind strike with the harpoons and run the lines out. The whale then rushes forward, and must be driven into the nets. Then a wild scene ensues, and every effort is made to surround the whale that is making frantic efforts to escape. He often does escape; but if he does not, he is soon surrounded by nearly three hundred naked yelling men, who throw harpoons and stones in such numbers that the huge prey is overcome. It is really an awful as well as pitiable sight; for the noble animal until very weak makes furious efforts to escape, rushing forward and coming up again to beat the sea into a bloody foam, at times smashing the boats or overturning them; and above all the din and yelling of the men, can often be heard the plaintive cry of the whale as the deadly weapons sink deep into his flesh. Before the whale is dead, and while he is rushing forward, a man with a very sharp knife leaps on his back near the head, and slashes two great gashes into the flesh, and passes a large rope several times around in the flesh, leaving a loop on the outside; the same kind of loops are made in the flesh nearer the tail. This is done in order that the whale may be tied up between two large boats to beams stretched across, and thus kept from sinking when he dies. In this way he is carried in triumph to the shore. The operation of cutting the holes and putting in the ropes is only done by the bravest and most skilful men. While the holes are being cut and the ropes passed in the man must hold on to the whale, and even go down with him into the water if he dives; for if he lets go, he is liable to be struck by the whale's tail and killed. The only thing to do is to tuck his head down and cling to the animal by the holes he has cut. He cannot raise his head, because he will at once be blinded by the water being driven into his eyes. When the fight draws to a close and the huge mammal is dying, all the whalers pray out Joraku! Joraku! Joraku! in a low deep tone of voice. Again, on the third day after the whale is taken, a memorial

service is held and prayers offered for the repose of the departed soul. If a baby whale is captured, a special *matsuri* (festival) is held on the ninth day afterwards. As soon as the whale is landed he is cut up, and it is a fearful sight; for the men strip themselves of all clothing, and hack and cut like madmen, all yelling at the same time with the greatest excitement. Some men even cut holes and go bodily into the whale, and, coming out all covered with blood, look like horrid red devils. . . .

Most Western visitors to Japan were obliged to subsist, at least in part, on local food. Few seem to have relished this fare and many recorded disparaging comments about it. But these do not amount to systematic information about Japanese diet, a central feature of the culture so many had come to observe and experience. An early source of such data is the Descriptive Catalogue *prepared by the Sanitary Bureau of the Japanese Home Department for the International Health Exhibition held in London in 1884. This not only contains valuable, if incomplete, statistical information but also much detail on methods of preserving and using some of the most common foodstuffs, the techniques of which appear to have escaped the notice, and certainly the comprehension, of western observers:*

Rice

Rice . . . is an indispensable means of subsistence . . . It would be one of the most important topics to describe exactly the amount of rice grown and the quantity consumed, but as no exact returns have been obtained, the general outline may be stated as follows . . . the people who eat rice daily is 53 per cent of the whole inhabitants. But other classes of people, such as farmers, eat such food stuffs as barley, *awa, hiye, kibe* (3 kinds of millet), sweet potato &c., instead of rice.

Maidenhair Tree Fruit (Ginnan)

An acrid poison is contained in this fruit; such that if the poisonous juice touches the body, boils will immediately be produced. Should any one eat it raw, he will soon be affected by its poison, but when roasted, its poisonous qualities disappear entirely, and there has never been a single case of poisoning known to arise from its use when roasted.

Mushroom (Shii-take)

The method of growing mushrooms is the following: – Various tall trees are cut down, marks are made by knives, and the trees left for two years upon the ground. On a winter day the timber is cut into pieces and the logs left inclining to a fence, or made into square piles and left alone from two to four years. Mushrooms then begin to grow in rainy season. They are afterwards covered over, and the full-grown ones are picked . . . The gathered mushrooms are compressed with bamboo sticks and dried by exposure to the open air or to fire.

Use – Dip into cold water or warm water for some time. Boil with soy, sugar or 'mirin' (a kind of sweet liquor) etc., or serve with soup.

'Katakuri' Starch

Preparation – The bulb of Erythronium dens-canis is crushed, washed with water, and decanted. The precipitated starch is collected, spread upon mats, dried by exposure to the sun, and finally ground into fine powder.

Use – It is made into something like vermicelli, called 'Katakuri men', and is chiefly used as a material for

making confectionery, or made into paste by adding hot water. It is served with sugar and makes very delicious food.

Laver, Dried Asakusa-nori

Method of gathering – The period for gathering laver is the latter part of September. The twigs of the Ho (Magnolia hypoleuca), of the oak, or of the Keyaki (Zelkowa Keaki) are made up into faggots, which are placed upon the bottom of the sea, at low tide, and after 30 to 40 days the weeds grow round the faggots. After severing it from the faggots, it is thoroughly washed several times, in order to remove the dirt clinging to it, and then it is put into tubs and cleaned with pure water. After it is thoroughly cleansed, it is dipped out of the tub with a grain measure, spread on a raised stand . . . that has been previously covered with bamboo screens. To prevent the substance from running over each screen is surrounded with a rim.

The weed is left until all the water has oozed away. The rim is then removed and . . . the (laver) is picked off and exposed to the rays of the sun, after which it is stored . . .

Use – To prepare the cured weed for table, it is placed over a fire and dried, and then eaten with rice; it has a very delicious bouquet and flavour, and is highly esteemed by every one.

Miso (a fermented substance made from Soy Beans)

Preparation – . . . The usual mode is, after soaking soy beans in water for about two hours, to put them into a suitable vessel and steam them; then, after mixing them with salt and yeast, they are removed to wooden plates; the next step is to evenly mix the ingredients. The liquid is then put into casks, and is then left untouched for upwards of a year.

Use – In Japan miso is one of the most necessary articles of food, and has been used from time immemorial, both by nobles and men of inferior rank. It is made into a soup, and is one of the courses served up as a principal article of every day diet. The mode of making it into soup is, in the first place, to rub it around an earthen ware bowl, into which a suitable quantity of water has been poured; it is then filtered through a sieve . . . and vegetables according to taste are added to it; the whole is then boiled and served up . . . The uses of miso are innumerable and it is most delicious food.

Katsuwobushi (dried bonito)

Katsuwobushi is made of the bonito, which is caught from July to October, at a distance of from 10 to 25 miles out at sea.

Mode of preparation – It is prepared by drying the fish, after it has been divided into four long strips, with artificial heat. During the process of drying there are many steps to be taken. Katsuwobushi undergoes no change from variations to temperature, and can be preserved for several years. It has been well known, from ancient times, that it is suitable for sea voyages, and for military campaigns.

Use – To prepare it for eating it is planed into thin shavings with a carpenter's plane; sometimes it is pul-

Tea became a major export item

verized and then boiled with a moderate quantity of salt. It is used as a condiment with boiled rice to which it gives such a delicious flavour that it suits the palate of every one. It also excites the secretions of the salivary glands and assists digestion. Sometimes it is chewed and swallowed, and it then affords considerable nourishment; moreover, it is an established fact that it allays the pangs of hunger and is stimulating, and the Japanese have great admiration for it.

The Descriptive Catalogue provides information on more than three hundred types of food and drink. Tinned foods available by the 1880s in Japan included bamboo shoots, mushrooms, turnip, radish, carrots, kidney beans, ginger, burdock, lotus root, brake fern and 'field horse tail'. The entry for 'Shochiu', a strong spirit made from the left-overs of sake-brewing, informs the reader that it is not only a favourite summer drink but also 'used as a medicine or for dressing wounds.' The universal liking for tea in Japan is explained on the grounds that it 'revives the spirits . . . allays the ennui incidental to old age, and promotes sociability.' The virtues of the pickled salted plum, if less frequently invoked, are no less remarkable:

If Umeboshi (pickled plum) is preserved in an earthenware jar and sealed up tight, with a thick paper cover, it will keep for over ten years. It is very valuable as a provision in campaigns and on voyages. Moreover, its taste remains unchanged even to the palates of those suffering from high fever or those whose sense of taste from the same cause has been much impaired: therefore it is kept in almost every house, and is especially used for invalids.

Intrigued visitors to the Exhibition need not confine the satisfaction of their curiosity to reading the catalogue or examining the hundreds of exhibits, for, on the upper floor of (appropriately enough) the Eastern Arcade, there was a Japanese restaurant with the following set menu on offer:

MISOSHIRU – Miso soup
KUCHITORI – Side dish
HACHIMONO – Grilled, stewed or roast
CHOKU – Dressed Vegetables
HAN – Boiled Rice
WANMORI – Soup of Fish or Meat with Vegetables
SUNOMONO – Vegetables, salted or preserved in Miso
SAKE – Japanese Wine
CHA – Japanese Tea
Foreign Wines Extra
SASHIMI (raw fish) – 'Very common food in Japan, will be served on special notice.'

And in addition to the above:

Japan Tea Rooms are open daily from 11 a.m. in the Garden of the London Water Companies' Pavilion. There are served to the visitors Japanese Green and Black Tea.

The 1884 International Health Exhibition was broad in its remit and the Japanese exhibitors responded eagerly to the opportunity to present as many aspects of their way of life as were compatible with the theme of the occasion. Apart from the food and drink section there were some three hundred items of clothing and accessories, ranging from straw rain-coats and tooth-pick holders to naval uniforms and traditional court costume, plus full-size clothed models of 'A Couple of the Ancient Samurai Class with their Daughter', 'A Couple of Well-To-Do People in Ordinary Attire', 'A Couple of Tradesmen Dressed in Their Ordinary Clothes', 'A Couple of Farmers Dressed in Working Dress', 'Falconer's Dress', 'Fireman's Dress' and half a dozen others. Housing was represented by scale models of urban and rural homes, a tea-ceremony house, a stable and a tenement, specimens of drain pipes and a portable urinal, of stoves and kitchen utensils, lanterns, vases and fitments. A twentieth-size model of a public bath-house and some forty associated items illustrated the

'Cleanliness is one of the few original items of Japanese civilisation . . . Ceremonial purifications continue to form part of the Shinto ritual. But viewed generally, the cleanliness in which the Japanese excel the rest of mankind has nothing to do with godliness. They are clean for the personal satisfaction of being clean. Their hot baths . . . also help to keep them warm in winter . . . cleanliness is more esteemed by the Japanese than our artificial Western prudery. As the editor of the Japan Mail has well said, the nude is seen in Japan, but not looked at.'

Basil Hall Chamberlain

'. . . their justice is severely executed without any partiality upon transgressors of the law. They are governed in great civilitie. I meane, not a land better governed in the world by civill policie.'

William Adams, 1611

'. . . three Japonians were executed . . . which done, every man that listed came to trie the sharpenesse of their cattans (katana meaning swords) upon the corps, so that before they left off, they had hewne them all three into peeces as small as a man's hand, and yet notwithstanding did not then give over, but placing the peeces one upon another, would try how many of them they could strike through at a blow; and the peeces are left to the fowles to devoure.'

Captain John Saris, 1613

significance attached by the Japanese to personal cleanliness, while the frugality and ingenuity induced by centuries of poverty and overcrowding was documented by a careful account of recycling procedures for:

Disposal and Utilization of Sewage and Refuse

Night Soil – A certain person has the removal of night soil from every house, and such matter is removed from closets at certain fixed periods, the matter being applied to the fields as manure.

Dirty Water – The dirty water from kitchens or from baths is led into drains distant from the dwelling-house, or is made to flow into a cesspool in the corner of the garden (in some places). It is used as manure for crops.

Refuse of Rice – It is given to dogs, fowls, sparrows etc. or is thrown into dirt heaps.

Refuse of Fish – This is given to cats or dogs, or thrown into the cesspool in the corner of the garden, wherein it is kept as manure for trees and shrubs.

Refuse of Vegetables etc. – What the cattle can eat is given to them as fodder . . .

Smoke – Windows on the roof of houses are open, and from them the smoke, especially of the kitchen, issues; and what remains in the house is used for drying bamboos to preserve them from decay.

Ashes – These are used for cleaning oily metallic or earthen plates; also as lye for washing and cleaning under-shirts etc . . .

Waste Paper – Waste paper is sold to those engaged in the business, and is resold to paper makers, who pulp it up for *Sukigayeshi* (paper made of waste paper).

Rags – This kind of refuse is sold to indigo makers, who extract the colouring matter by boiling the rags, and make indigo of it; the residue is thrown upon dirt heaps, and also used for paper manufacture of European system.

Broken Articles – Certain kinds of broken pieces of pottery are, after grinding up, used as material for manufacturing other pottery mixed with fresh material. Also pieces of broken glass-ware are used for making glass again, by melting them. As to lacquered or gold-lacquered articles, the gold is scraped off, and then what is left is burned . . .

Other Japanese exhibits included an army field ambulance, a display of 'Meteorology in its Relation to Public Health' and an entire section on the new national education system, complete with models of school buildings, gymnastic apparatus, origami, class-room equipment, specimens of pupils' work and embroidery and over three hundred text-books.

The Mikado *was first performed on 14 March 1885. According to Rutland Barrington, one of the principal players:*

Never during the whole of my experience have I assisted at such an enthusiastic first night as greeted this delightful work. From the moment the curtain rose on the Court swells in Japanese willow-plate attitudes to its final fall it was one long succession of uproarious laughter at the libretto and overwhelming applause for the music . . .

Sir Arthur Sullivan recorded rapturously in his diary:

New opera *The Mikado* or *The Town of Titipu*, produced at the Savoy Theatre with every sign of real success. A most brilliant house. Tremendous reception . . . Seven encores taken – might have taken twelve.

The reviews were, however, mixed. According to the Evening News *the Gilbert and Sullivan partnership was clearly flagging and their latest offering 'was not likely to add very much to the reputation of either author or composer.' And, while* The

THE ELECTRIC BELL
will ring in the
ROYAL BARS,
In Grey Street and Market Street,
adjoining the Entrances to the Theatre,
3 MINUTES
Before the rising of the Curtain for
EACH ACT.

GIBSON & CO.,   PROPRIETORS.

STYLISH MILLINERY.
LADIES SHOULD VISIT

S. PITTS,
28, NUN ST., NEWCASTLE,
For LATEST FASHIONS AS PRODUCED.
PRICES STRICTLY MODERATE.

MONDAY, SEPT. 6th, 1886,
And Every Evening during the Week, at 7·30,

THE

MIKADO!

OR, THE TOWN OF TITIPU.

Written by W. S. GILBERT.   Composed by ARTHUR SULLIVAN.

The Mikado of Japan .... Mr. ALLEN MORRIS

Nanki-Poo (his Son, disguised as a Wandering Minstrel, and in love
with Yum-Yum)....................... Mr. CHARLES HILDESLEY

Ko-Ko (Lord High Executioner of Titipu) ...... Mr. GEORGE THORNE

Pooh-Bah (Lord High Everything Else) .... Mr. JAMES DANVERS

Pish-Tush (a Noble Lord) .... Mr. GEORGE GORDON

Yum-Yum ...   Three Sisters, ... Miss ETHEL PIERSON
Pitti-Sing ...   Wards of Ko-Ko   ...... Miss HAIDEE CROFTON
Peep-Bo ...   . Miss SIDDIE SYMONS

Katisha (an elderly lady, in love with Nanki-Poo) Miss FANNY EDWARDS

Chorus of School Girls, Nobles, Guards, and Coolies.

ACT I.

COURTYARD OF KO-KO'S OFFICIAL RESIDENCE.

ACT II.

KO-KO'S GARDEN.

The Incidental Dances by Mr. J. D. AUBAN.

The Ladies' Dresses by Messrs. LIBERTY & Co., and Madame LEON.

The Gentlemen's Dresses designed by Mr. WILHELM, from Japanese
authorities, and executed by Madame LEON.

The Wigs by Mr. CLARKSON.

Acting Manager.........   ....Mr. R. REDFORD
Musical Director ......   For   ...... Mr. GEORGE ARNOLD
Stage Manager ....   Mr. D'Oyly Carte   ...... Mr. R. WEATHERSBY

MONDAY, SEPTEMBER 13th, 1886,

The Eminent Comedian,

MR. EDWARD TERRY

Supported by his SPECIALLY SELECTED COMPANY.

Athenaeum *conceded that 'the score of the new opera exhibits Sir Arthur Sullivan at his best' it also regretted that 'so much ability should be employed on productions which from their very nature must be ephemeral.'* Theatre *took the plot altogether too seriously and accused its creators of being:*

. . . unsusceptible of a single kindly feeling or wholesome impulse; were they not manifestly maniacal they would be demoniacal . . . Decapitation, disembowelment, immersion in boiling oil or molten lead, are the eventualities upon which their attentions are kept fixed, with gruesome persistence . . .

Actor-manager Henry Irving, whose judgement was more definitive than a thousand critics, would have none of this carping and hailed it as 'the greatest triumph of light opera, British or foreign.'

And he was right. The Mikado *ran for another 671 performances, establishing a record for a London run which was to last for almost forty years.*

Nor was its success limited to Britain. Its charm seemed destined to cross every boundary of culture and taste. It took America by storm and inspired a host of imitators and pirate productions. By 1886 there were no less than five officially approved companies on tour there and on one particular night it was estimated that there were no less than 170 separate performances going on simultaneously across the United States and Canada.

Nor did language prove a barrier. The prestigious All-gemeine Musik Zeitung praised The Mikado *for:*

. . . numbers of a quite extraordinary richness and of a fine quality heretofore absolutely unknown in our operetta.

It was swiftly translated into German, Czech, Serbo-Croat and Hungarian.

How can such success be explained? The Athenaeum *came nearer to most in finding an answer:*

Mr Gilbert has once more exhibited his facility for seizing upon a subject and turning it to humorous account. Japanese art is extremely fashionable just at present . . .

'It seems to me quite fortunate that the musical art is not more generally practised.'

Alice M. Bacon, 1891

The Daily Telegraph *concurred that 'We are all being more or less Japanned.' And* The Musical World *in its review, laid special emphasis on the fact that:*

All were delighted with the beauty of the costumes, appointments and scenery.

Indeed they were right to be, for Gilbert had paid scrupulous attention to this aspect of the production and the very first stage direction of the libretto requires that the scene should open with:

Japanese nobles discovered standing and sitting in attitudes suggested by native drawings.

But why the interest in Japan?
  Gilbert himself confessed in an interview at the time that:

I cannot give you a good reason for our forthcoming piece being laid in Japan.

Though he did point out that:

. . . to lay the scene in Japan afforded scope for picturesque treatment, scenery and costume . . .

A decade later he gave the New York Tribune *a much more fanciful story:*

In May 1884 it became necessary to decide upon a subject for the next Savoy opera. A Japanese executioner's sword hanging on the wall of my library – the very sword carried by Mr Grossmith at his entrance in the first Act – suggested the broad idea upon which the libretto is based. A Japanese piece would afford opportunities for picturesque scenery and costumes, and, moreover, nothing of the kind had ever been attempted in England.

The sword incident may have been crucial – or merely incidental. But it is also interesting to note that, at the very moment Gilbert was searching for a novel theme – May 1884 – the Cornhill Magazine *carried an anonymous account of a visit to 'The Capital of the Mikados', which contained three of the essential features of life in 'Titipu'. First there was the brilliance of the 'native costume':*

A peacock is nothing to a Kioto girl out for the day.

Secondly there was the notion that Japan itself was somehow not just another place but another planet:

. . . judging from the behaviour of the natives, I should say that the average of Europeans finding their way thither in the course of a year is small . . . wherever we went there assembled a crowd of people . . . They were very quiet and not intentionally rude, but their capacity for a long, steady stare is infinite . . . They did not whisper or point . . . They just stood and dumbly stared, watching every slightest motion or gesture of the strange beings who had dropped from heaven knows where upon the streets of their city.

And finally there was the notion of the awesomeness of the Mikado himself:

. . . it is impossible to turn in any direction without being confronted with evidence of the reverence with which the person of the Mikado was regarded . . . The Mikado was, in considerable measure yet is, more than a human being.

As Gilbert set to work on the libretto fate conspired to bring Japan to his very doorstep with the construction at Knightsbridge, less than a mile from his Kensington home, of an entire Japanese village. This remarkable venture was the work of one 'Tanakker Buhicrosan' who succeeded in securing royal and noble patronage

for his project and pledged himself to use its profits to forward the cause of Christianity in his native land. The January 1885 number of Nature *was enthusiastic in a guardedly patronizing sort of way:*

The undertaking to transport a whole Japanese village, with its shops, houses and inhabitants, half round the globe to London, was a somewhat bold one for a private individual . . . The houses are new and clean, which the tenements of Japanese villages always are not; the small temple or shrine is rather more cleanly and ornamental than is usual with these structures in real life; the wrestlers do not exhibit the physical characteristics which are so conspicuous, not to say disgusting, in the real Japanese wrestler; and their methods of refreshing themselves between the bouts are more in accordance with European tastes . . . There is very little to note in the exhibition from a scientific point of view; the inhabitants are fair average specimens of Japanese artisans and shopkeepers, so that the ethnologist will have a good opportunity to comparing his notions gathered from Miss Bird and other writers of the Japanese people with the reality. He can, in a measure, study the racial chacteristics of the Japanese *in situ*.

A month later, within three weeks of the opening night of the The Mikado, *the even more widely-read* Illustrated London News *gave a full page to the exhibition and its 120 inhabitants, complete with nine drawings of its principal attractions:*

The almond-eyed artisans are encamped in Humphrey's Hall, Knightsbridge, and look most wonderfully at home there. The planks for their shops, the platforms on which they sit, or rather squat, and the low desks, or tables, at which they work, have all been brought over bodily; and if only the sunshine, the blue sky, and the tropical foliage could have been added, the picture of Japanese life would have been perfect. As it is, the men and women evidently enjoy the joke immensely, glance up at their visitors with quick, bright eyes, make remarks about them to one another in their strange, but not unmusical, tongue, and go on with their work in the unhasting yet unresting manner which so eminently distinguishes the oriental from the western races. Their long brown hands do not look over clean, and they hold their tools in what seems to us an unhandy fashion, but the effects they produce are true and neat and exquisitely finished . . . The Japs tuck their feet up under them in the most comfortable fashion . . . and a sound of barbaric, but not discordant, music comes in single notes from the annexe, where a vocal and instrumental performance is going on.

Our Artist has made Sketches in the tea-house, where the cup that cheers is handed to you by a damsel who half hides her laughing face with her loose sleeve . . . and, again, at the umbrella-maker's shop, where the bamboo framework rests on a sort of easel while the maker turns it round, covers it with paper, and paints the surface with grotesque figures. Further on there is a tray and cabinet maker: and in a recess between two shops there is something like a temple, or at all events an inclosure devoted to a hideous idol, before which two lanterns burn continually . . . The single-stick and theatrical performances attract large numbers of spectators but the most abiding interest seems to be that taken in the shops and artisans.

Gilbert's reliance on this source for technical guidance was prominently acknowledged in the premiere programme:

The Management desires to acknowledge the valuable assistance afforded by the Directors and Native Inhabitants of the Japanese Village, Knightsbridge.

There were other highly competent sources of assistance as well. Liberty's of Regent Street, which had already established firm trading links with Japan and numbered the Japanophile artist, Whistler, among its customers, supplied the costume fabrics. And for final touches of authenticity Gilbert could always appeal to a near neighbour in Harrington Gardens, who was none other than A.B. Mitford, an authority on 'the Happy Dispatch' if ever there was one.

After a brief interval The Mikado *was revived in 1888, received the accolade of a command performance at Balmoral in 1891, and was revived again in 1895, 1896 and 1904. In 1907, however, it became the focal point of a political row as splendidly absurd as its own plot. The Lord Chamberlain, whose varied duties included that of being Britain's offical theatre censor, announced that* The Mikado *would be banned indefinitely to avoid offending Crown Prince Fushimi, who was shortly to make a state visit to the United Kingdom. He was supported in this by a letter to* The Times *from Joseph Longford, who had served for over thirty years as a British consul in Japan:*

The production of *The Mikado* was from the first an insult to the most sacred sentiments of the Japanese, galling and humiliating in every way.

He was backed up in turn by Lord de Saumarez, a former Secretary to the British Legation in Tokyo:

. . . the very name given to this play is offensive to the feelings of every Japanese, whatever disclaimer any individual Japanese, actuated by the national somewhat exaggerated politeness, may verbally make when assaulted by an interested interviewer.

When Gilbert pointed out that the ban, somewhat inconsistently, did not extend to army and navy bands playing music from the score – the ban was promptly extended to cover them as well. In the House of Commons the Prime Minister was asked whether he intended to ban Hamlet *in future because it might offend the royal house of Denmark, the family of the King's own consort.*

Ironically an official of the Japanese embassy seemed entirely unoffended by the alleged offensiveness of the disputed work and stated:

I am deeply and pleasingly disappointed. I came . . . expecting to discover real insults to my countrymen. I find bright music and much fun, but I could not find the insults . . . I envy the nation possessing such music. The only part of the play to which objection might be taken is the presentation of the Mikado on stage as a comic character. This would be impossible in Japan . . . there is nothing else to criticize from the national point of view, but there are other things which a Japanese would say. I cannot understand from what part of Japan the author got the names of his characters . . . Of course, the play shows quite an imaginary world, not in the least like Japan. The characters embrace and kiss quite publicly. In my country this would be quite shocking . . . I had a pleasant evening, and I consider that the English people, in withdrawing this play lest Japan should be offended, are crediting my country with needless readiness to take offence.

The ban was withdrawn after six weeks and Gilbert was knighted in the same year, observing mischievously that shortly:

. . . we shall probably be at war with Japan about India and they will offer me a high price to permit *The Mikado* to be played.

The enduring popularity of The Mikado *depends, of course, not on its painstaking, but entirely superficial Japaneseness, but on its Englishness. As G.K. Chesterton so succinctly put it:*

There is not, the whole length of *The Mikado*, a single joke that is a joke against Japan. They are all . . . jokes against England . . . The Mikado is not a picture of Japan; but it is a Japanese picture.

In 1886 a Captain Grierson prepared an appreciation of the new Japanese army for the British war office. His overall conclusion was to damn the achievements of two decades with faint praise:

The army of Japan is quite good for Asia but it could not stand up to European troops as its men lack the true military instinct.

According to the traveller and man of letters, Wilfred Scawen Blunt, such views were not universal:

General Descharmes talked much of Japan, where he was military instructor for some years . . . He declares them to have *le diable dans le corps* for fighting, and that it would take a European power all it knew to beat them. 'I would not,' he said, 'undertake to land an army in Japan with less than 60,000 men, all Frenchmen.'

Major Henry Knollys of the Royal Artillery, author of Sketches of Life in Japan, *devoted a chapter of his book to* 'Notes on the Japanese Army', *although he disarmingly warned in a footnote that:*

The non-military reader is warned that most of this chapter is of a technical nature. He may therefore prefer to skip it.

Major Knollys' perceptive and humorous analysis shows a Victorian army officer who is anything but the splenetic and narrow-minded martinet of popular imagination. Not the least of his virtues as a commentator was his determination to judge what he saw by the highest professional criteria:

I preface the details of my experience, however, by remarking that I should be paying them an exceedingly bad compliment were I to give tongue to that unmixed applause so often applied by those who call themselves the best friends of the Japanese, but who are in reality their worst enemies. I should in that case be clearly, though unavowedly, judging them by the standard of semi-civilization.

The strongest proof which I can furnish of my appreciation is to apply a European standard to an army which is absolutely in its childhood, which a few years ago consisted of little more than hordes of imperfectly-equipped, almost barbarously-armed fighting men, but which in an astonishingly short space of time has, thanks to an almost magical intelligence and enterprise without parallel in the annals of military history, emerged into the civilized efficiency of modern armies . . . the manifest condition of my using truly this standard is, that I must find much to criticise relatively, however great my constant inclination to applaud absolutely.

That said, Knollys also warns the reader that:

. . . the Japanese, sensitive to a degree of European

Soldiers of Japan's modern army in action against the 'Boxers', 1900

criticism, especially shrink from being taken unawares and
without due preparation, lest they should not show off at
their best. This susceptibility entails one great evil, which
is so characteristic of their models, the French – the evil
that their theory and their actuality are incessantly at
variance . . .

*Knollys regarded Japanese official statistics for the strength of
their army as exaggerated and found many branches of the service
to exist only in embryo:*

. . . the actual effectives are far below the nominal strength
. . . There are no siege train or garrison batteries. Neither
is there a regular commissariat corps. The functions of this
department are undertaken by civilian contractors. A
Telegraph and Medical Staff Corps have been established,
but are still in their infancy . . . A sort of embryo Staff
College has been established . . . but . . . their staff is
furnished from Regimental Officers, temporarily told off
for the duty . . .

The bulk of the new army consisted of infantry:

The men stand as steady in the ranks as well-trained
English or German troops. No low murmur of voices or
shuffling of feet, or wriggling of heads, such as is the
almost invariable concomitant of troops of southern
climes standing ostensibly 'at attention'.
    The clothing, which is blue and bears a first cousinship
to the French uniform, the arms and equipment, are all in
good order, and well turned out in every respect. But as
regards physique, they strike one as conspicuously dwarf-
ish – too small, in fact, for their weapons – and no wonder,
inasmuch as their average height barely exceeds five feet.
Moreover, they appear deficient in what I may call muscular solidarity . . .

*Officer cadets likewise struck Knollys as lacking that certain
soldierly something:*

My first reflection is that the gulf between them and the
lower classes is comparatively narrow . . . The cadets look
very clean, quiet and intelligent. So do nineteen out of
twenty ordinary Japanese. But their voices, manner, and
general aspect, physical and otherwise, differ but slightly
from the ruck . . . Their drill is tolerable but spiritless, and
without the pleasant, though sometimes troublesome,
vivacity of high-spirited boys. Only in the gymnastic
exercises is there a trace of boy humour, when the squads,
scaling an escarp and parapet, break into strange cries and
swarm up perpendiculars with monkey-like agility . . .
the curriculum of study possesses a general affinity to that
pursued by European military schools, though of a much
lower standard.

*An inspection tour of barracks proved revealing to the practised
and sceptical eye:*

. . . my conducting party were incessantly adjuring me to
make every possible inquiry . . . I more than suspect that
this invitation is mere talkee-talkee . . . But still . . . there
can be no real discourtesy . . . if I take them at their
word. . . .
    'How many boots has the private soldier?'
    'Two pairs. One pair he wears, and the other he keeps at
his bed-head.'
    'Why,' I reply, 'I do not see that second pair belonging
to yonder man.'
    'Oh, gone to be mended.'
    'But,' I urbanely suggest, 'I do not see a single second
pair among all the thirty men in the room.'
    Baffled silence – and I hastily change the subject.
    'Can you please tell me what are the articles of his kit?'
    A long enumeration which comprises the most liberal

'They are of nature very proper in their behaviour . . .'

St Francis Xavier, 1549

supply of every item conducive to cleanliness, health and comfort.

'Now,' I coaxingly entreat, 'would you be so kind as to permit me to see the nature of these articles? May that man, for instance, unpack his squad bag?'

Dismayed hesitation – but there is no help for it. And I have some difficulty in maintaining my gravity as a French officer . . . standing close by, mutters with a keen sense of the ridiculous, mingled perhaps with a little vexation, *'Dieu sait ce qu'il y trouvera.'* 'Ah – I thought so: a blanket, shirt and head-dress, a piece of some nasty eatable, and a box of flea-powder. The theory and practice of the regulations differ widely; and I only mention the above trivialities to show that in Japan, as in the French army, a scratch on the surface often reveals essential deficiencies in what is so fair-seeming.

But where credit was due, Knollys proved keen to give it:

The hospital arrangements, if rather embryonic, are surprisingly good, considering the depths of native medical ignorance . . . The regimental stores are kept in a praiseworthy orderly manner, though they are scanty in quantity . . . We might, with advantage, copy their large wash-houses, with numerous hip-baths and an unlimited supply of hot water. Soldiers, no matter what their nationality, never can be persuaded to face freely cold water . . . The kitchens, too, are admirable; but then the cooks are not bothered with any complexities as to variety of diet.

In the matter of discipline Knollys regarded the Japanese as, if anything, too perfect:

Their general good behaviour is quite extraordinary. The assertions that there is no insubordination, absence without leave, drunkenness, making away with kit, and breaking out of barracks, might possibly be called in question, were it not that my careful search for lock-up prisoners'-rooms, cells, defaulters, prisoners and record of offences was totally without result – in fact I am persuaded that none such existed.

It may be urged how incalculably advantageous must be this absence of crime. I am not so clear . . . for the conviction is hourly growing on me that the Japanese private soldier is over docile, over obedient . . . Better surely that he should occasionally insult his sergeant-major, knock down his sergeant, break out of barracks and make away with his kit, than show evidence of a lack of spirited impetuosity which constitutes so valuable a component of a soldier.

Watching cavalry in action, Knollys thought them scruffy in turn-out but impressive in manoeuvre. As for artillery, his own special sphere of expertise:

It is in no respect even approximately as good as the English artillery – but this is no dispraise . . . The Japanese field batteries will not suffer by comparison . . . with those of France, Belgium or Prussia. Indeed, the special arm seems to have called forth the special and advantageous characteristics latent in the nation.

This last naturally leads on to a consideration of weapons manufacture and ordnance supply, a field in which the Japanese had chosen Italy as their model, though British example also had some influence, as Knollys gathered from a Colonel Mourata:

. . . whose one object of adoration was 'Ooritch', which, as it dawned on my mind at the end of our interview, was his rendering of 'Woolwich'.

Knollys was also gratified to learn that all high-quality iron was imported from Britain and:

I note a satisfactory testimony to the excellence of our machinery in the fact that nearly all the apparatus, huge and minute, bear the stamp: 'Whitworth, Birmingham'.

Perhaps unfortunately in Knollys' view, it went no further:

The Japanese, in the same way that they selected England as a model for their navy, engineering works, postal and telegraphic administrations, Italy for the construction of ordnance, America for public education, and Germany for medicine, selected France for the army. Her system is French to the very core; French in dress, interior economy, and to a great extent in language. French, in a fair show not always coexistent with reality, and French in many of its virtues and most of its vices.

Few acts can have been more symbolic of Japan's determination to emulate the West than the decision in 1873 to oblige courtiers and government officials to adopt western dress when on duty. The ebullient Japanophile, Arthur Diosy, chronicled the resulting sartorial revolution with sympathy and enthusiasm:

From 1873 to 1887 . . . the adoption of European dress progressed rapidly amongst the upper classes . . . and had steadily gained ground amongst students, bankers, merchants, and others coming, more or less directly, under foreign influence.

The wave of German influence that swept over Japan from 1885 to 1887 carried the innovation to a still more dangerous point. The beautiful costume of the women of Japan, so absolutely becoming to its wearers that one can hardly imagine them clad in any other way, was threatened, and sad to relate, the ladies of the Court began to order dresses from – Paris? No – the pen almost refuses to chronicle the appalling fact – *from Berlin!* In the nick of time, the reaction against a Slavish imitation of Occidental customs unsuited to the country came to the rescue. In 1887, the national spirit, roused to indignation against the Western powers by the failure of Count Inouye's attempts to induce them to negotiate a Revision of the Treaties on the basis ardently desired by the Japanese, caused a sudden return to many of the old habits and customs that had fallen into abeyance . . .

Its outward and visible sign is the resumption of their picturesque and becoming national dress by both men and women of the upper class. The uniforms, naval, military and civil, are all of European patterns; so is the court dress of the nobility – more is the pity, for no statelier costume could be devised than that worn by the nobles of Old Japan – and, at most of the court functions, the Empress, one of those gracious little *grandes dames* who look charming and dignified in any costume, appears in European dress, together with her ladies, some of whom now accustomed to wear it, wear it with truly Parisian grace. Officials are clad in European costume during office-hours, but it may be safely said that, with the above exceptions, the Japanese of the upper class now wear their national dress at all times when the nature of their work, or recreation, does not render Western clothing much more suitable.

Diosy's admiration for Japanese 'national dress' is almost unqualified and curiously buttressed by his eagerness to find parallels with European styles:

The dress of the Japanese civilian . . . is simple in cut, sombre in colour, neat to a degree, and in excellent taste. The wide-sleeved silken gown, or *kimono*, of some quiet, dark colour, in very narrow vertical stripes divided by black lines, showing at the breast where the left side is crossed over the right, the edge of an undergarment of precisely similar cut, perhaps the edges of two such undergowns . . . these edges . . . showing in a manner

Golden Pavilion, Kyoto. After surviving five centuries of wars, earthquakes and fires it was burned down by a monk in 1950

'This country is hilly and pestered
with snow wherefore it is neither
so warm as Portugal not yet so
wealthy . . .'

R. Willes, 1565

that recalls the superimposed waistcoats of a past generation in Europe. Over the *kimono*, the wide *hakama*,
commonly translated by 'trousers' but really a divided
skirt, of sober-coloured silk – probably of some bluish-
grey tint with narrow vertical black stripes, strikingly
similar to the 'striped Angola trouserings' of the fashionable London tailors. The *obi*, or girdle, of thick silk, four
yards long and two and three-quarter inches wide, is
smoothly and evenly wound about the waist. Over all, the
haori, or overcoat, of stiff, black corded silk, tied across the
breast by two silken cords, slung in a graceful loop, the
back of the coat, just below the collar, and the sleeves
bearing the wearer's crest, his *mon*, beautifully embroidered in white silk, within a circle of about the size of a
shilling.

These garments compose a costume which proclaims in
its tasteful simplicity that it is the dress of a gentleman of
refinement. And, indeed the impression is confirmed by
closer examination; it is borne out by every outward sign,
from the crown of the hatless head to the small, well-
shaped feet, still free from the painful deformities caused
by the irrational foot-gear of Western civilization, and
encased in the most comfortable, hygienic covering
imaginable, the strong, soft-soled socks, generally white,
called *tabi*, which have a separate compartment for the big
toe . . .

*Diosy's rapturous approbation is, however, offset by his pained
observations on the subject of head-gear and haircuts:*

The Japanese gentleman has been described as hatless.
Would that this were always true, or that, at all events . . .
he would wear one of the various shapes of shady, light,
and cool hats, of straw, or of split and plaited bamboo,
used in summer by the labouring classes and wayfarers,
the kind most in favour amongst them being an inverted
bowl . . . with a light inner rim fitting round the head, on
the principle of the 'sun-helmets' used by Europeans in the
tropics, a perfectly rational, hygienic hat! Unfortunately, his
natural good taste seems to fail him at times, and he sees no
incongruity in wearing, with his graceful, dignified silken
costume, any sort of Western head-gear, from the jaunty
'Homburg hat' of grey or brown felt . . . or of straw, with its
cleft crown, or the hard, low-crowned 'bowler', to the straw
hat of the Occidental boating-man, and even – sad to relate! –
to that abomination of modern Britain – the shapeless cloth
'stable-cap' with its peak of the same material, or sometimes, more hideous still, the double-peaked, ear-flapped,
'fore-and-aft' cap of sad-coloured cloth.

. . . He wears his abundant hair cut in the Occidental
fashion, not always, sooth to say, in the most approved
Bond Street or Piccadilly style – too frequently, an
inverted pudding-basin would appear to have guided the
scissors in their course – but, uneven or sleek, his hair,
with its *parting* in the European fashion, is a sign of the
Great Change.

*Rudyard Kipling was utterly charmed when he visited Japan in
1889 as part of a world tour:*

It is strange to be in a clean land, and stranger to walk
among dolls' houses. Japan is a soothing place for a small
man.

As well as being soothed he was also on occasion hugely amused:

Nagasaki is inhabited entirely by children. The grown-ups
exist on sufferance. A four-foot child walks with a three-
foot child, who is holding the hand of a two-foot child,
who carries on her back a one-foot child, who – but you
will not believe me if I say that the scale runs down to
six-inch little Jap dolls such as they used to sell in the
Burlington Arcade. These dolls wriggle and laugh. They

Foreign flags and bowler hats denote the 'internationalization' of Japan

'. . . *dressed only in one's virtue . . .*'
Rudyard Kipling

are tied up in a blue bed-gown which is tied by a sash, which again ties up the bed-gown of the carrier. Thus if you untie that sash, baby and but little bigger brother are at once perfectly naked. I saw a mother do this, and it was for all the world like the peeling of hard-boiled eggs.

But sometimes the joke was on him:

Had I been sheltered by the walls of a big Europe bath, I should not have cared, but I was preparing to wash when a pretty maiden opened the door, and indicated that she too would tub in the deep, sunken Japanese bath at my side. When one is dressed only in one's virtue and a pair of spectacles it is difficult to shut the door in the face of a girl. She gathered that I was not happy, and withdrew gig-

gling, while I thanked heaven, blushing profusely the while, that I had been brought up in a society which unfits a man to bathe *à deux*. . . .

Kipling seems to have been sure that the Japanese were superior to the Chinese, but couldn't really define how:

The Chinaman's a native . . . that's the look on a native's face, but the Jap isn't a native, and he isn't a Sahib either.

Kipling also convinced himself that, unlike the Chinese, the Japanese lacked commercial acumen and should stay clear of trade:

The Japanese should have no concern with business. The Jap has no business savvy.

Indeed, he fantasized:

It would pay us to establish an international suzerainty over Japan: to take away any fear of invasion and annexation, and pay the country as much as ever it chose, on condition that it simply sat still and went on making beautiful things while our learned men learned. It would pay us to put the whole Empire in a glass case and mark it Hors Concours, Exhibit A.

The countryside, however, was living proof of the industriousness of the Japanese. Travelling by train between Kobe and Osaka, Kipling and his travelling companion were clearly staggered by what they could see gliding by:

Imagine a land of rich black soil, very heavily manured, and worked by the spade and hoe almost exclusively, and if you split your field (of vision) into half acre plots, you will get a notion of the raw material the cultivator works on. But all I can write will give you no notion of the wantonness of neatness visible in the fields; of the elaborate system of irrigation, and the mathematical precision of the planting. There was no mixing of crops, no waste of boundary in footpath, and no difference of value in the land. The water stood everywhere within ten feet of the surface, as the well-sweeps attested. On the slopes of the foot-hills each drop between the levels was neatly riveted with unmortared stones, and the edges of the water-cuts were faced in like manner. The young rice was transplanted very much as draughts are laid on the board; the tea might have been cropped garden box [i.e. box hedge]; and between the lines of the mustard the water lay in the drills as in a wooden trough, while the purple of the beans ran up to the mustard and stopped as though cut with a rule.

Tea growing on the hills and rice on the plains

'This is a child's country. Men, women and children are taken out of the fairy books. The whole show is of the nursery.'

Henry Adams, 1886

On the seaboard we saw an almost continuous line of towns variegated with factory chimneys; inland, the crazy-quilt of green, dark-green and gold. Even in the rain the view was lovely, and exactly as Japanese pictures had led me to hope for. Only one drawback occurred to the Professor and myself at the same time. Crops don't grow to the full limit of the seed on heavily worked ground dotted with villages except at a price.

'Cholera?' said I, watching a stretch of well-sweeps.

'Cholera,' said the Professor. 'Must be, y'know. It's all sewage irrigation.'

The port of Kobe showed Kipling the face of a new Japan, which repelled him:

We walked down the wide, naked streets, between houses of sham stucco, with Corinthian pillars of wood, wooden verandahs and piazzas, all stony grey beneath stone grey skies, and keeping guard over raw green saplings miscalled shade trees. In truth Kobe is hideously American in externals. Even I, who have only seen pictures of America, recognised at once that it was Portland, Maine.

American influence in general came in for singularly forthright condemnation:

There are many American missionaries in Japan, and some of them construct clapboard churches and chapels for whose ugliness no creed could compensate. They further instil into the Japanese mind wicked ideas of 'Progress' and teach that it is well to go ahead of your neighbour, to improve your situation, and generally to thresh yourself to pieces in the battle of existence. They do not mean to do this; but their own restless energy enforces the lesson. The American is objectionable.

A decade later Kipling was married to an American and living in America!

Like many visitors before and since, Kipling was prompted by what he saw and experienced to reflect upon his own British identity, reaching a conclusion which ingeniously contrived to be both modest and immodest at the same time:

Japan is a great people. Her masons play with stone, her carpenters with wood, her smiths with iron, and her artists with life, death and all the eye can take in. Mercifully she has been denied the last touch of firmness in her character which would enable her to play with the whole round world. We possess that – We, the nation of the glass flower-shade, the pink worsted mat, the red and green china puppy dog, and the poisonous Brussels carpet.

It is our compensation.

Writing of Mount Fuji in 1962 the English poet James Kirkup confessed rather testily:

I once started to climb it, in company with about a million Japanese, but it was so unpleasantly like scrambling up a pile of coke that I gave up after five minutes.

'As time goes on, he [Fuji] becomes an infatuating personality.'

Isabella Bird, 1878

'A lucky day is chosen for the wedding. When it comes, the bride, dressed all in white, the colour of mourning – to signify that she dies to her own family, and that she will never leave her husband's house but as a corpse – is borne away at nightfall to her new home . . . The wedding, which takes place immediately on the bride's arrival . . . is of the nature of a dinner party . . . When it is added that a Japanese bride has no bridesmaids, that the young couple go off on no honeymoon, that a Japanese wife is not only supposed to obey her husband, but actually does so, that the husband, if well enough off, probably has a concubine besides and makes no secret of it, and that the mother-in-law, with us a terror to the man, is not only a terror but a daily and hourly cross to the girl . . . it will be seen that marriage in Japan is a vastly different thing . . .'

Basil Hall Chamberlain

'Together with the Sun-goddess, numerous other deities, commonly spoken of as "the eight-hundred myriads of gods," are worshipped . . . These multitudinous deities govern all things . . . Their worship is very general . . . Every village, town or division of a town has its patron deity and common temple, and the inhabitants of the district are called the children of the god, and bring their infant children to be dedicated to him. When the local festivals are held, business is often suspended, and each householder hangs a large lantern at his door in honour of the god.'

Church Missionary Society, 1905

Kirkup's Victorian predecessors were made of sterner stuff. The first British assault on the sacred mountain was led by Sir Rutherford Alcock, brusquely ignoring the uncomprehending protestations of the Minister for Foreign Affairs, who told him that:

It was not fitting in a person of the rank of a British envoy to make the pilgrimage, limited by custom if not by law to the lower classes!

The humility of the true pilgrimage spirit was perhaps conspicuous by its absence on this particular occasion for, on attaining the summit, the party:

. . . unfurled the British flag, while we fired a royal salute from our revolvers in its honour, and concluded the ceremony by drinking the health of Her gracious Majesty in champagne, iced in the snows of Fuji-yama.

That was in 1860. Thirty years later when Sir Edwin Arnold made the ascent such expeditions had become both more acceptable for visitors and much easier to organize. It had not, however, been reduced to a routine tourist experience and demanded exertion which it duly rewarded with exhilaration:

You would not wonder, residing here, that everybody in Japan talks about Fuji, and thinks about her; paints her on fans, and limns her with gold on lacquer; carves her on temple-gates and house-fronts, and draws her for curtains of shops and signboards of inns, rest-houses and public-institutions . . . you would soon perceive how the great volcano dominates every landscape, asserts perpetually her sovereignty over all other hills and mountains, and becomes in reality as well as imagination, an indispensable element in the national scenery.

    . . . It is a circuit of 120 miles to go all round the base of Fuji-San. If you could cut a tunnel through her . . . it would be forty miles long. Generally speaking, the lower portion of the mountain is cultivated to a height of 1,500 feet, and it is a whole province which thus climbs round her. From the border of the farms there begins a rough and wild, but flowery moorland, which stretches round the hill to an elevation of 4,000 feet, where the thick forest belt commences . . . Above the forest extends a narrow zone of thicket and bush . . . after which comes the bare, burnt, and terribly majestic peak itself, where the only living thing is a little yellow lichen . . . for no eagle or hawk ventures so high . . .

    The best – indeed, the only – time for the ascent of the mountain is between July 15th and September 5th. During this brief season, the snow will be melted from the cone, the huts upon the path will be opened for pilgrims, and there will be only the danger of getting caught by a typhoon, or reaching the summit to find it swathed day after day in clouds and no view obtainable . . .

    Such an expedition may be divided into a series of stages. You have first to approach the foot of the mountain by train or otherwise, then to ride through the long slope of cultivated region. Then, abandoning horse or vehicles, to traverse on foot the sharper slopes of the forest belt. At the confines of this you will reach the first station, called Sho or Go; for Japanese fancy has likened the mountain to a heap of dry rice and the stations are named by rice measures. From the first station to the ninth, whatever road you take, all will be hard, hot, continuous climbing. You must go by narrow, bad paths, such as a goat might make, in loose volcanic dust, gritty pumice, or over the sharp edges of lava dykes, which cut boots and sandals to shreds.

Starting at day break and accompanied by six porters to carry their bedding and provisions, Arnold and his companions reached Station No. 4, at 8,420 ft, by 9.30 a.m. and paused for a well-deserved breakfast:

It is already welcome enough to halt and shake the sharp ashes from our boots, while we drink Liebig essence in hot water and eat tinned meats with an appetite sharpened by the already keen air. But we have a great height yet to climb to No. 6 station, where we shall lunch, and the path henceforward is of two kinds – both abominable. Either you zigzag to and fro in the loose black and red ashes, too steep and slippery to climb directly; or you pick your way over the rugged slag and clinkers of a lava dyke, which is like ascending a shattered flight of steps or climbing the face of a furnace bank. Every fifteen minutes one or other of the strong mountaineers accompanying us cries out, 'O ya-sumi!' and we all sink gladly on the nearest block, breathing quick and hard, the air being now so rarified that it seems impossible to get enough into the lungs.

After each rest, of a minute or two, we plod on towards the little black lava hut marked by fluttering red and white flags, which is our next goal; and truly very far off, and very high up, and very hard to reach each in turn seems to be . . . Nevertheless, early in the afternoon we do reach Station No. 8, where we shall pass the night, more than 11,000 feet above sea-level. Not only is the air very rarefied, but also very cold . . . All vegetation has vanished . . . and we are glad to unpack our blankets and lie under them round the hibachi, while such a meal as the mountain hut can furnish is being prepared. It consists of little else than small salted fish fried upon rice, but we supplement it with tinned provisions, and wash it down with weak whiskey and water . . .

The shortest time in which the ascent has been made is six hours and a half. We, taking it more easily, made no attempt to beat the record, and stopped frequently to botanize, geologize etc. The rareifaction of the air gave our Japanese companion, Takaji San, a slight headache, which soon passed . . but Captain Ingles and I, being I suppose, both in excellent health and strength, experienced no inconvenience worth mentioning.

The view from the hut at dawn moved Arnold to a lyricism which quite transcends the gruff, no-nonsense style of his narrative:

I looked out, almost as you might from the moon, over a prodigious abyss of space, beyond which the eastern rim of all the world seemed to be on fire with flaming light. A belt of splendid rose and gold illumined all the horizon, darting long spears of glory into the dark sky overhead, gilding the tops of a thousand hills, scattered over the purple plains below, and casting on the unbroken background of clouds beyond an enormous shadow of Fuji. The spectacle was of unparalleled splendour, recalling Lord Tennyson's line:

'And, in the East,
God made himself an awful Rose of Dawn.'

Moment by moment it grew more wonderful in loveliness of colour and brilliant birth of day; and then, suddenly, just when the sun rolled into sight – an orb of gleaming gold, flooding the world beneath with almost insufferable radiance – a vast mass of dense white clouds swept before the north wind over the view, completely blotting out the sun, the belt of rose and gold, the lighted mountains and plains, and the lower regions of Fuji-San. It was day again, but misty, white and doubtful . . .

After that the actual summit was almost an anticlimax.

Lafcadio Hearn (1850–1904) was probably more influential than any other single writer in English in developing the image of Japan as a 'lotus land' of Fuji and flowers, geishas and ghosts, although, like most 'classic' writers on a subject, he was probably far more widely quoted in scraps than read in depth.

Lafcadio Hearn was a writer in English, but was he an English writer? His father was Anglo-Irish, his mother was Maltese and he was born on the Greek island of Lefcada, from

'The mountain which I found higher to climb than I had heard, than I had thought, than I had seen – was Fuji's peak.'

Kada-no-Azuma-Maro, Japanese poet

'Natives and foreigners, artist and holiday-makers, alike fall down in adoration before the wondrous mountain which
stands utterly alone in its union of grace with majesty.'

Basil Hall Chamberlain

which he took his unique name. At the age of seven he was adopted by an elderly aunt whose idea of a proper upbringing was alternately to spoil him and immure him in Catholic seminaries. At one of these he suffered a sports injury which blinded him in one eye and caused the other to bulge out grotesquely, leaving him obsessed by his own appearance – until he reached Japan, where all Westerners were regarded as weird-looking anyway.

Shy, and introspective, but with a precocious appetite for the off-beat and bizarre, as a young man Hearn set himself to become a writer. In Cincinnati, Ohio, where a black woman became his common-law wife, he wrote prodigiously for local journals and translated reams from French writers, who were to exert a formative influence on both his choice of subject-matter and his style. Slaving to 'polish' his descriptive prose or short stories, he achieved results which strike the modern reader as awkwardly mannered – what even one of his sympathetic biographers, Edward Thomas, called 'a cumbrous English, stiffened with beauties which do not make it beautiful.'

Drifting through New Orleans, Hearn moved on to the French West Indies, gradually convincing himself that only in some such exotic clime could a person of his 'Latin temperament' feel at ease – 'One lives here. In New Orleans one only exists.'

In 1890 Hearn accepted a commission from Harper's Weekly *to visit Japan to write a series of travel sketches. When he arrived he knew at once that his odyssey was at an end. Throwing up his commission, he accepted a post as an English teacher in the town of Matsue. So sure was his conviction that he had at last found his rightful place in the universe he composed a lengthy essay on* My First Day in the Orient', *which set out, as it were, a preliminary itinerary for his voyage of discovery:*

The traveller who enters suddenly into a period of social change – especially change from a feudal past to a democratic present – is likely to regret the decay of things beautiful and the ugliness of things new. What of both I may yet discover in Japan I know not; but today, in these exotic streets, the old and the new mingle so well that one seems to set off the other. The line of tiny white telegraph poles carrying the world's news to the papers printed in a mixture of Chinese and Japanese characters; an electric bell in some tea-house with an Oriental riddle of text pasted beside the ivory button; a shop of American sewing-machines next to the shop of a maker of Buddhist images; the establishment of a manufacturer of straw sandals; all these present no striking incongruities, for each sample of Occidental innovation is set into an oriental frame that seems adaptable to any picture. But on the first day, at least, the Old alone is new for the stranger, and suffices to absorb his attention. It then appears to him that everything Japanese is delicate, exquisite, admirable – even a pair of common wooden chopsticks in a paper bag with a little drawing upon it; even a package of tooth-picks of cherry-wood, bound with a paper wrapper wonderfully lettered in three different colours; even the little sky-blue towel with designs of flying sparrows upon it, which the jinricksha man uses to wipe his face. The bank bills, the commonest copper coins, are things of beauty. Even the piece of plaited coloured string used by the shopkeeper in tying up your last purchase is a pretty curiosity. Curiosities and dainty objects bewilder by their very multitude: on either side of you, wherever you turn your eyes, are countless wonderful things as yet incomprehensible.

Such unqualified enthusiasm could not last – and it didn't. Disillusion and despair assailed, but their victories were seldom lasting. Indeed, few writers can ever have taken identification with their subject further than did Hearn. He married a Japanese wife and was adopted into her family, assuming the name Koizumi Yakumo and achieving Japanese citizenship in 1896. And, although he never learned enough Japanese to enable him to read a newspaper properly, and could only just manage a simple letter home, he won the respect of his long-time correspondent, the eminently expert Basil Hall Chamberlain, who observed that:

Bronze: 'the metal in which Japanese art was already winning its brightest laurels over a thousand years ago.'
Basil Hall Chamberlain

Lafcadio Hearn understands contemporary Japan better and makes us understand it better, than any other writer, because he loves it better.

Meanwhile the books poured out of him. His initial delight in the juxtaposition of the new and the old was increasingly replaced by an obsession with the fragility and preciousness of a past that was daily slipping away beneath a rising tide of western materialism:

. . . how utterly dead Old Japan is, and how ugly New Japan is becoming.

The very titles that Hearn chose for his writings are indicative of his overpowering sense of transience – Glimpses of Unfamiliar Japan, Out of the East, Exotics and Retrospectives, In Ghostly Japan, Shadowings.

Although Hearn often seems to communicate with his reader in a confidential, even confessional, tone, his deepest anxieties and forebodings were expressed in his private correspondence, especially with Basil Hall Chamberlain:

At first the sense of existence here is like that of escaping from an almost unbearable atmospheric pressure into a rarefied, highly oxygenated medium. That feeling continues: in Japan the law of life is not as with us, – that each strives to extend his own individuality at the expense of his neighbour's. But on the other hand how much one loses. Never a fine inspiration, a deep emotion, a profound joy, or a profound pain, – never a thrill, or, as the French say so much better than we, a *frisson*.

I think we have thrown Japan morally backward a thousand years: she is going to adopt our vices (which are much too large for her).

Imagine people having no sentiment of light – of blue infinity! And they cannot possibly feel beauty of their own day as you or I do. I think of the comparison of Fuji to a white half-open inverted fan, hanging in the sky: of course it is pretty; it is even startlingly real; – but what sentiment is there in it? What feeling do mountains give this people?

The development of the mathematical faculty in the race – unchecked and unmollified by our class of aesthetics and idealisms – ought to prove a serious danger to western civilization at last . . . Imagine a civilization on western lines with cold calculation universally substituted for ethical principle! The suggestion is very terrible and very ugly. One would prefer even the society of the later Roman Empire.

Hearn, of course, conceived an intense dislike of Tokyo, the booming, bustling heart and symbol of 'New Japan':

In this Tokyo, this detestable Tokyo there are no Japanese impressions to be had except at rare intervals. To describe to you the place would be utterly impossible – more easy to describe a province. Here the quarter of the foreign embassies, looking like a well-painted American suburb; – nearby an estate with quaint Chinese gates several centuries old; a little further square miles of indescribable squalor; – then miles of military parade-ground trampled into a waste of dust, and bounded by hideous barracks; – then a great park full of really weird beauty, the shadows all black as ink; – then square miles of streets and shops, which burn down once a year, – then more squalor; – then rice fields and bamboo groves; – then more streets. All this not flat but hilly – a city of undulations. Immense silences – green and romantic – alternate with quarters of turmoil and factories and railroad stations. Miles of telegraph poles looking at a distance like enormous fine-tooth combs, make a horrid impression. Miles of water-pipes, – miles and miles and miles of them – interrupt the traffic of the principal streets: they have been trying to put them

'Here, remember, the people really eat lotuses; they form a common article of diet.'

Lafcadio Hearn, 1891

'Owing to the narrowness of the country, most Japanese streams are rather torrents than rivers.'
Basil Hall Chamberlain

'But how sweet the Japanese woman is! – all the possibilities of the race for goodness seem to be concentrated in her.'

Lafcadio Hearn, 1891

underground for seven years . . . Streets melt under rain, water-pipes sink, water-pipe holes . . . swallow up playful children; frogs sing amazing songs in the street. – To think of art or time or eternity in the dead waste and muddle of this mess is difficult.

That careless rapture which so delighted in the combination of the old and new had by now long departed. Even Hearn's experiences as a teacher had begun to fill him with frustration:

Here is an astounding fact. The Japanese child is as close to you as a European child – perhaps closer and sweeter because infinitely more natural and naturally refined. Cultivate his mind, and the more it is cultivated the farther you push him from you. Why? – Because here the race antagonism shows itself. As the Oriental thinks naturally to the left, where we think to the right, the more you cultivate him, the more he will think in an opposite direction from you.

Although as a teacher, and perhaps even indirectly as a writer, Hearn was shaping the character of the new Japanese elite, he tended to shun the ruling class of eager modernizers whose iconoclasm was so often applauded by Western visitors. Instead Hearn valued:

. . . the great common people, who represent in Japan, as in all countries, the national virtues and who still cling to their delightful old customs, their picturesque dresses, their Buddhist images, their household shrines, their beautiful and touching worship of ancestors.

This last was to strike a particularly resonant chord in Hearn's battered soul. He had struggled for years to reject the harsh religious upbringing which had infected him with a morbid fear of the agonies of hell and a mistrust of beauty and sensual pleasure. Searching for a substitute philosophy, he had been profoundly impressed by the post-Darwinian theories of Herbert Spencer. When Hearn began his researches into the religious heritage of Buddhism and Shinto, he found traditional notions of the transmigration and transmutation of souls to be, as Louis Allen has so deftly put it, 'sheer evolutionary common sense', which complemented rather than conflicted with the revelations of modern science. Japan's spiritual culture also provided a comprehensible context for what Hearn took to be one of the most fundamental features of its society – 'the rule of the dead.'

In brief, he asked:

Is not every action indeed the work of the Dead who dwell within us?

Reverence for ancestors implied not only the physical continuity of a genetic inheritance but the psychological continuance of a moral authority underpinning the state itself:

Only religion could enable any people to bear such discipline without degenerating into mopes and cowards; and the Japanese never so degenerated: the traditions that compelled self-denial and obedience, also cultivated courage, and insisted upon cheerfulness. The power of the ruler was unlimited because the power of the dead supported him.

Hearn's appreciation of this novel perspective on the universe continued to find expression in passages which were perhaps extravagant, or even whimsical, as, for example, in this discourse on dust from Gleanings in Buddha Fields:

Assuredly this dust has felt. It has been everything we know; also much that we cannot know. It has been nebula and star, planet and moon, times unspeakable. Deity also it has been . . . Thou hast been Light, Life, Love; – and into all these, by ceaseless cosmic magic, shalt thou many times be turned again! . . . This earth must die; her seas

'While many of them are poor, poverty is held to be no disgrace.'
St Francis Xavier, 1549

Nagoya after an earthquake, 1891

'The Japanese have done with their past.'
Basil Hall Chamberlain

shall be Saharas. But those seas once existed in the sun; and their dead tides, revived by fire, will pour their thunder upon the coasts of another world. Transmigration, transmutation: these are not fables! What is impossible? . . . Resurrection there is, – but a resurrection more stupendous than any dreamed of by Western creeds. Dead emotions will revive as surely as dead suns and moons.

This revelation was not only universal but individual in its implications:

I, an individual; an individual soul! – Nay, I am a population – a population unthinkable for multitude, even by groups of a thousand millions. Generations of generations I am, aeons of aeons! Countless times the concourse now making me has been scattered, and mixed with other scatterings. Of what concern, then, the next disintegration? Perhaps, after trillions of ages of burning in different dynasties, the very best of me may come together again.

The summation of Hearn's views is to be found in his modestly titled Japan: An Attempt at Interpretation, *published shortly before his death. Of its twenty-two chapters more than half are concerned with religion or matters which – like the structure of the family – Hearn considered to have a fundamentally religious basis or dimension. Although he had seen much to deplore in his adopted country Hearn still saw it as a land in which:*

. . . every relation appears to be governed by altruism, every action directed by duty and every object shaped by art.

Anticipating stinging criticisms from 'real sociologists', Hearn feared that he might have been in error to depart from his customary subject:

. . . birds and cats, insects and flowers, and queer small things.

He need not have worried. The poet and critic Edward Thomas hailed Hearn's masterpiece as:

. . . probably the best single book, not a work of reference, upon Japan . . . an extraordinary effort . . . to express what one man could not possibly grasp, especially one who knew, as he said himself, enough about Japan to know that he knew nothing.

Hearn's stature was such that within a decade of his death there had appeared a two volume Life and Letters, *a separate edition of his correspondence and three shorter 'appreciations' of his life and work. Perhaps the tribute that would have gladdened him most came from his Japanese biographer, who praised him as a truly Japanese writer:*

. . . in perfect accord with the sweet glamour of Old Japan . . . the old romances which we had forgotten ages ago were brought again to quiver in the ear and the ancient beauty which we buried under the dust rose again with a strange yet new splendour.

If Kipling thought the Japanese ought to stay out of business, so did the American T.R. Jernigan, but for rather different reasons:

They (European merchants) complain . . . not so much of actual, wilful dishonesty . . . as of pettiness, constant shilly-shallying, unbusinesslikeness almost passing belief. Hence the wide divergence between the impressions of the holiday-making tourist and the opinions formed by the commercial communities at the open ports. Japan, the globe-trotter's paradise, is also the grave of the merchant's hopes.

'. . . mountainous and craggy, full of Rockes and stonie places . . .'

Arthur Hatch, 1623

Jernigan's observations are to be found in his book on China's Business Methods and Policy. *He, like many others, was struck by the contrast between two peoples who were often confused with each other by Europeans and Americans who lacked first-hand experience of the region:*

Another deep-seated difference between the Chinese and the Japanese is that the former have race pride, the latter national vanity. The Chinese care nothing for China as a political unit . . . but they are nevertheless inalienably wedded to every detail of their ancestral civilisation. The Japanese, though they have twice, at intervals of a milennium, thrown everything national overboard, are intense nationalists in the abstract. In fact, patriotism may be said to be their sole remaining ideal. No Chinaman but glories in the outward badges of his race; no Japanese but would be delighted to pass for a European in order to beat Europeans on their own ground.

One of the prime reasons for 'opening' Japan was to gain access to her markets. The preoccupations of Stafford Ransome's Japan in Transition, *published in 1899, show that after forty years this was still no easy matter. Ransome, an engineering consultant and economic journalist, devoted an entire chapter of his work to 'The Commercial Integrity of the Japanese'. He began by looking at the problem from the point of view of an entrepreneur approaching the market for the first time:*

It is to be presumed that, as a rule, the business visitor to Japan has made some attempt to study his subject more or less before he leaves his country . . . The consular reports will afford him conclusive proof that business, a large and increasing business, is being done with Japan. The London merchant, while confirming that fact, will add that, while it may be just as well for him to go out to see for himself

how the trade is done, he would strongly advise him to fight shy of dealing direct with the Japanese, for their business methods are strange.

The business man who has previously visited Japan will endorse and emphasise the opinion of the merchant. He will say that the Japanese in business are devoid of integrity . . .

The somewhat puzzled business man goes to Japan, and talks to the treaty-port people. He is told that the Japanese are all dishonest; that they repudiate their contracts; that they will put him to no end of trouble in getting him to give them estimates and particulars; that they will, generally speaking, suck his brains; and that, if he is unfortunate enough to receive an order from them, they will certainly have no intention of paying for the goods when they have been delivered. That, in a few words, is the gist of the treaty-port opinion of Japanese business morality.

Ransome tried to put this discouraging impression in a larger context:

Political and administrative integrity in Japan is undoubtedly high. It is not of course ideal, but, comparing Japan with many countries whose civilisation has been brought about by the slow growth of ages, the methods of her politicians and statesmen are less open to reproach than those of half the countries in Europe, to say nothing of those of the Western hemisphere. Again the lower classes, the smaller tradesmen, servants, and so, with the exception perhaps of those in and near treaty-ports are, as such people go in other countries, distinctly honest. To account for the alleged dishonesty of the Japanese in their dealings with the local foreigner, we must remember that as a nation they have until quite recently been a fighting, an artistic and an agricultural rather than a trading people, as we understand the word. In Japan, not so long ago, a trader was a person to be treated with contempt; and,

The 'opening' of Japan led to a huge increase in foreign trade, which ran ahead of the development of modern port facilities. Here traditional boats are used for cargo-handling

After 1868 new official holidays celebrated the Emperor

when a certain class is habitually looked down upon in any country, that fact is not at all conclusive to a high code of morals in the methods of the men of that particular class . . .

The Japanese of the present day follow the current literature of Europe and America very closely, and they can see enough in the journals of many civilised countries to convince them that colossal financial and commercial swindles are in many well-known centres quite the order of the day. Then again in their dealings with the foreigner it has not always been the latter who has been the honest man in the transaction: and while, as a rule, the Japanese have been as well served as one could expect, they have undoubtedly from time to time individually and collectively been robbed by some of the people from whom they have acquired their impressions of Western business methods.

Ransome's own explanation for trading difficulties was primarily a cultural one:

. . . I believe that most of the unsatisfactory transactions have been due to a misunderstanding on both sides, rather than to a want of honesty on either side.

We must bear in mind, on the one hand, that the foreign treaty-port trader neither reads nor writes Japanese, and that, with rare exceptions, he does not even speak the language sufficiently well to carry on an intricate negotiation satisfactorily; and on the other, that the Japanese purchaser has not always been able to know whether he was applying to a specialist in a particular line or not, and that he often did not know what he was purchasing. The result is that both parties have been in the hands of a Japanese business tout, who might or might not be an honest man, and who might or might not be a capable man, if he happened to be honest. These facts, more than any other, have been responsible for the widespread impression as to the general want of integrity among Japanese business men.

Looking to the future the author predicted great changes:

Personally I anticipate that the rapid growth of the Japanese mercantile marine, and the wonderful extension of the ramifications of the big Japanese merchant firms in all corners of the earth, will, in the course of time, have the effect of ousting the foreigner to a very marked degree; for there are few foreign firms that have the wealth necessary to compete against the Japanese merchants successfully in the long run.

These changes, properly understood, could still afford opportunities for profitable business:

. . . if . . . the days of the trading foreigner in Japan are numbered, it does not necessarily follow that the international business of the country will decline. Nor does it necessarily mean that business foreigners will not be needed in that country. The channels through which Japanese orders find their way to the manufacturer may be changed, and the orders may not in every case find their way to their present destinations. Consequently, it behoves manufacturers who wish to retain their Japanese trade to find out for themselves the best steps to be taken to secure that end.

Now the business foreigner of whom the Japanese are in want – although they do not, as a rule, acknowledge the fact – is the thoroughly technical man . . . They will not engage him and pay for him themselves, because, in their present ultra-nationalist frame of mind, they like to feel that they can do without him. It may, however, pay some of our larger manufacturers to send over to Japan at their own expense men who thoroughly understand the details of their particular specialities, who will be in a position to

The development of Japan's navy and merchant marine greatly strengthened Anglo-Japanese links as Japan looked to Britain both for ships and training

Refuelling a modern liner with hand-carried baskets of coal

tell the Japanese what they want to know. The ordinary commercial tout, whatever his value might have been in Japan years ago, is distinctly at a discount now. The Japanese business people have a good insight into modern business methods; they have their banking establishments all over the world; and they know how to make estimates, and how to quote for most of the ordinary articles of commerce at the present day. But what they do not altogether know is how to select the makers of the foreign articles they require, and they are constantly misled by the catalogues of inferior and even bogus manufacturers . . .

Ransome concludes his analysis with a plea and a warning that is as relevant today as when he wrote it a century ago:

. . . the great stumbling-block to satisfactory trade with Japan is the want of knowledge of the Japanese language by our traders. Over and over again I have heard it said that it is quite useless to speak Japanese because so many of them speak English. In fact, the Europeans who speak Japanese fluently seldom or never make use of it when talking to a Japanese who speaks their language even imperfectly, unless he is an intimate friend; as it is said that the Japanese resent the use of their language by a foreigner. But the fact remains that the man who is not able to understand the language of the party he is dealing with is often at a very great disadvantage in carrying on an intricate negotiation.

In stating this I am aware that I am laying myself open to criticism that to suggest that a knowledge of Japanese should be attained by our local traders is to suggest an impossibility. But, if this is so, it means that the Japanese must hold the whip-hand over the foreigner in commerical matters in their own country.

The British Government, which is not particularly noted for the break-neck speed with which it rushes ahead of the times, has long since grasped the fact that it is necessary that its local diplomatic and consular officials should speak Japanese . . .

The business man will tell you, and possibly he is right, that life is not long enough to permit of an exhaustive study of Japanese. If that is so, it is to be feared that, from the moment that the Japanese have completed their modern education, the foreign trader, who once was placed on a pedestal, and, who, if not liked, was, at all events, regarded with profound respect on account of his wonderful knowledge, will have lost all his prestige, and with it his chances of carrying on his business at a profit . . .

By the turn of the century tourism in Japan had become sufficiently well-developed for the standard Handbook for Travellers in Japan *to have achieved its sixth edition. First drafted by the eminent diplomat Sir Ernest Satow, it had been assiduously revised by the scholarly Basil Hall Chamberlain – 'Emeritus Professor of Japanese and Philology in the Imperial University of Tokyo' – with the assistance of W.B. Mason – 'Late of the Imperial Japanese Department of Communications'. The* Handbook's *advice inadvertently reveals much about the habitual concerns and demeanour of the Victorian visitor to Japan as well as being, in many respects, sound counsel to this very day:*

In Japan, more than in any Western country, it is necessary to take some trouble in order to master . . . preliminary information; for whereas England, France, Italy, Germany and the rest, all resemble each other in their main features, because all alike have grown up in a culture fundamentally identical, this is not the case with Japan. He, therefore, who should essay to travel without having learnt a word concerning Japan's past, would run the risk of forming opinions ludicrously erroneous . . . In any case a supply of books of some sort is indispensable to help to while away the frequent rainy days . . .

A guide is an absolute necessity to persons unacquainted

with the language. Those knowing a little Japanese may feel themselves more their own masters by hiring a man-servant or 'boy' also able to cook, and having neither objection to performing menial functions, nor opinions of his own as to the route which it will be best to take.

The Imperial Japanese Post and Telegraph services are excellent. Letters and papers can be forwarded with perfect safety to the different stages of a journey.

What is termed *hatago* at a Japanese inn includes supper, bed, and breakfast, for which a single charge is usually made . . . Scanty as the entertainment may often appear to one fresh from the innumerable luxuries of a comfortable European hotel, it should be remembered that such things as fine lacquer and porcelain utensils, painted screens, and silk quilts, to say nothing of numerous well-dressed attendants, are expensive items to mine host, and are charged for accordingly. Anything in the way of food or liquor ordered in addition to the meals supplied is considered an extra. There is no charge for firing, lighting, attendance, or bath, provided always the traveller is content with what is given to every one else, neither is there any for tea . . . It is but fair that foreigners should pay more than natives, both for accommodation and for jinrikishas. They usually weigh more, they always want to travel more quickly, they give infinitely more trouble at an inn with their demands for fresh water in the bath, the occupation of a portion of the kitchen to cook their European food in, and a dozen other such requirements, to say nothing of their insisting on having separate rooms, while Japanese guests – even strangers to one another – are habitually required to share a room together.

Though garments of the roughest description will suffice for the country districts, bring good clothes, such as might be worn at home, in which to appear at the larger hotels, and to mix, if need be, in society, whether Japanese or foreign. Japanese officials now attend their offices in frock or morning coats, and Europeans visiting them

should be similarly attended. At a few of the highest social functions, frock-coats and tall hats are expected. With regard to boots, it is advisable to wear such as can be pulled off and on easily, as it is necessary to remove one's boots every time one enters a house or temple, in order not to soil the mats on which the Japanese sit. Grave offence is given, and naturally given, by the disregard of this cleanly custom. . . .

At Yokohama, Chinese tailors attend the hotels, and will fit out travellers with duck, crape and other light clothing literally between a night and a morning. Washing is well and expeditiously done at the Open Ports and at the principal summer resorts.

Except at some of the larger towns and favourite hill or sea-side resorts, meat, bread and other forms of European food are unknown. Even fowls are rarely obtainable . . . Those, therefore, who cannot subsist on the native fare of rice, eggs and fish should carry their own supplies with them. Wines, spirits, aerated waters and cigars are equally unobtainable; but beer is met with in most towns . . . It is advisable to take one or two knives, forks, spoons, a corkscrew, a tin-opener and the most elementary cooking-utensils. Plates and glasses can be borrowed almost everywhere . . . Curry-powder will often help to make insipid Japanese dishes palatable, and shoyu (soy) adds a zest to soups . . . Many who view Japanese food hopefully from a distance, have found their spirits sink and their tempers embittered when brought face to face with its unsatisfying actuality.

Europeans usually avail themselves of the first-class railway cars . . . and ladies in particular are recommended to do so, as not only are the other classes apt to be overcrowded, but the ways of the Japanese bourgeoisie with regard to clothing, the management of children, and other matters, are not altogether as our ways.

If by 'doing' Japan be meant hurrying through its chief sights, the globe-trotter can manage this in three or four

'The wrestlers must be numbered among Japan's most characteristic sights, though they are neither small nor dainty, like the majority of things Japanese. They are enormous men, – mountains of fat and muscle, with low sensual faces and low sensual habits – enormous eaters, enormous drinkers. But their feats of strength show plainly that the "training" which consists in picking and choosing among one's victuals is a vain superstition.'

Basil Hall Chamberlain

'It is not dancing in our sense of the word, but posturing and dumb acting . . . The Japanese dance with everything but their feet. The story of the dumb show is told by the musicians, who not only tum-tum on the harp and sackbut and psaltery, but keep up a chant in a solemn and somehow not unmusical monotone, with cracked falsetto voices . . . The dances are just long enough to satisfy one, not long enough to be tiresome and we had sensations of genuine regret when the time came for us to order our jinrikishas and put on our boots.'

Douglas Sladen, 1908

weeks . . . He who is bent on more serious observation will not find four months too much; and one who has spent that time rarely fails to come again . . . travelling amidst . . . rough mountains is itself rough in the extreme. None but thoroughly healthy men, inured to hardship, should attempt it. The provincial towns have, for the most part, little individuality. As for what is called 'seeing Japanese life' the best plan is to avoid the Foreign Settlements in the Open Ports. You will see theatres, wrestling, dancing-girls, and the New Japan of European uniforms, political lectures, clubs, colleges, hospitals and Methodist chapels in the big cities. The old peasant life still continues almost unchanged in the districts not opened up by railways.

In the event of trouble arising . . . always apply to the police, who are almost invariably polite and serviceable. These officials must not be insulted by the offer of a tip. The same remark applies to railway guards and public servants generally.

Make your plans as simple as possible. The conditions of travel in this country do not lend themselves to intricate arrangements.

Take visiting cards with you. Japanese with whom you become acquainted will often desire to exchange cards. Above all, be constantly polite and conciliatory in your demeanour towards the people. Whereas the lower classes at home are apt to resent suave manners, and to imagine that he who addresses them politely wishes to deceive them or get something out of them, every Japanese, however humble, expects courtesy, being himself courteous. His courtesy, however, differs from that of the West in not being specially directed towards ladies.

Many travellers irritate the Japanese by talking and acting as if they thought Japan and her customs a sort of peep-show set up for foreigners to gape at . . . Too many foreigners, we fear, give not only trouble and offence, but just cause for indignation, especially in their behaviour

'All griefs can be assuaged by gazing at the moon'

towards Japanese women, whose engaging manners and naive ways they misinterpret . . .

Never show impatience. You will only get stared at or laughed at behind your back and matters will not move any quicker . . . It is best to resign yourself at the beginning, once for all.

Chamberlain and Mason's Handbook for Travellers *was intended for the discerning and thoughtful visitor. But there was another kind, a type which must have sent conscientious diplomats like the earnest authors of the* Handbook *running for cover as soon as they were sighted. One such was the author of* Three Rolling Stones in Japan *who achieves a level of sustained fatuousness that constitutes a genre of travel-writing all of its own.*

The opening paragraphs serve sufficient notice of the promise of the succeeding 250 pages:

That I might one day visit Japan has ever been one of my most pleasurable anticipations.

From the hills of desire I have all my life looked down on the Promised Land – as depicted on teacups, as sung in comic operas, or as traced with more prosaic accuracy on the map of the world. The possibility of posing in the society of some deliciously unnatural lady, upon a semi-circular bridge, seemed too bright a dream ever to come true. I often thought how I would enjoy making the acquaintance of the Japanese moon (a very superior satellite and by no means to be confounded with other and more ordinary moons) from the summit of some fantastic pagoda. It would be pointed out to me by a mothlike maiden, affectionate yet modest, whose very familiarity would be charmingly unfamiliar, and we would sit together and watch it soar upwards into the blue night lulled by the songs of Japanese love-birds . . . Still, to return to Japan, everything appertaining to it has always affected me pleasantly. Even the little Japanese gentlemen

whom I used to meet wandering about the streets of London were full of interest to me. The entire absence of expression on their unattractive faces coupled with the entire absence of their ladies gave me food for much speculation. Why would they trust us with neither?

Thus forewarned one still flinches at the unerring ability of the author to realize Chamberlain's and Mason's worst fears:

Nagasaki impressed us very favourably. Everyone was busy . . . Even the beggars were jolly fellows, and smiled at us with a quite unprofessional cheerfulness. It is a curious sensation to be accosted by a hilarious hunchback who shows you his hunch as if it were the best joke in the world, or to have your attention drawn to poor sightless eyes only by the merry grin which stretches beneath them. They cannot help it: cheerfulness is inherent in the race. It is impossible to take anything seriously in Japan; everything seems made on purpose to be laughed at.

Nagasaki produces a new butt for the visitors' humour in the shape of a rickshaw-man named Tomi, who, with more hospitality than circumspection, introduces his new acquaintance to his daughters:

They possessed impossible names, so difficult of pronunciation that we were filled with despair. Kingston's efforts to vanquish the difficulty provoked shouts of laughter from the entire party, including the two other rickshaw men who were sitting in the doorway.

'Oh, I say!' he expostulated. 'Can't we rechristen them and call them something decent and English? – something descriptive, you know; we ought to be able to find something if we put our heads together.'

'What have said in so muchee talk?' inquired Karakamoko politely.

'I'm going to give your sisters new names.'

'Oh! Ah! What will call them?'

'Gurgles and Giggles.'

'Engleesh name?' asked Tomi with some anxiety.

'Very English,' we assured him.

'Ha! Thank you.'

'Me too,' pleaded Karakamoko.

'You want an English name, too?'

'Muchee like.'

'Then you shall be called Caricature.'

'All same name,' she murmured in a dissatisfied tone.

'Not a bit of it – quite English.'

'What can mean?'

'Oh, it means something very clever and funny – make you laugh.'

It made some readers laugh, apparently.

Perhaps the author of Three Rolling Stones in Japan *was writing with his pen, rather than his tongue, stuck firmly in his cheek. The same cannot be said for the author of* An English Girl in Japan, *an account of the summer of 1902, by Ella M. Hart Bennett, based on her diary notes. The eighteen-year-old daughter of an English businessman, who was prominent enough to be invited to Imperial receptions, Miss Bennett was evidently familiar with a number of standard works on Japan, both classic (Siebold) and contemporary (Bird, Arnold); but she still displayed a consistent crassness which can only be pardoned on the grounds of her youth, though she prided herself on having 'more practical knowledge of life than was usual for one of my age.'*

One of Miss Bennett's first adventures was an expedition to 'a Japanese Harrogate' (i.e. a hot-spring spa) in the company of the daughter of another English businessman. Her conduct, when they arrived at their first over-night accommodation made Miss Bennett look like a model of tact and sensitivity:

We were escorted to our bedroom by the landlord. Either from mistaken politeness or curiosity, he declined to leave us, repeatedly bowing and apologizing for the want of comfort in his miserable establishment, and assuring us how highly he appreciated the honour of entertaining such distinguished guests. All this in the most excruciating English. Hints that we wished to retire to bed were of no avail; and at last Pauline, unable to restrain her impatience any longer, drew back the 'shoji' (sliding panel) and, with an imperious wave of her hand, pointed from our little tormentor to the door, and said: 'Go, wretch!'. This had the desired effect. He departed, bowing even lower than before, still murmuring to himself 'honourable distinction'. 'Well,' I said to Pauline as, closing the panel carefully, she turned towards me, 'what about Japanese politeness? I thought it was the only thing that really was important out here. You have put your foot in it.' Pauline's face was a study. Notwithstanding her manner, which was most impressive, she was at heart extremely nervous and highly strung. It was some time before I could assure her that doubtless the little man was quite as glad to go as we were to get rid of him, and that there was

'However many servants she may have in her employ, it is a woman's duty not to shirk the trouble of attending to everything herself.'

The Greater Learning for Women

no fear of his detaining us by force or showing any resentment.

At last, however, we settled ourselves as comfortably as we could on our 'futons' (Japanese mattresses) on the floor, and slept the sleep of the just . . .'

After such an introduction it is scarcely surprising that:

Pauline was rather anxious to pay a visit to the lepers, as she remarked, 'When one is in for a thing it is best to miss nothing.' But I stoutly refused to go. The memory of the poor, crippled, deformed and suffering creatures I had seen in the streets of Kusatzu was quite enough. In fact, I found sleep almost impossible that night. The groans of the unfortunate bathers rang in my ears, and my dreams were peopled with visions of horrors of every description.

The splendour and solemnity of an Imperial garden-party, however, overawed even the dismissive Miss Bennett:

Each Legation went in turn to felicitate the Emperor on his birthday and to bow to the Empress. All had to walk backwards out of the tent past the Court ladies and officials – not an easy task. With some the Emperor said a few words. His face when smiling lighted up, changing his morose expression to one of almost benevolence. I own to feeling horribly nervous when my turn came to be presented by our Minister's wife, and breathed a sigh of relief when I arrived safe and sound at the Royal tent without having utterly disgraced myself by tumbling over my train, or knocking down one of the little officials who were stationed at every available corner.

Perhaps her respectful attitude owed a little to an earlier startling experience:

I was standing in one of the streets to watch the Emperor

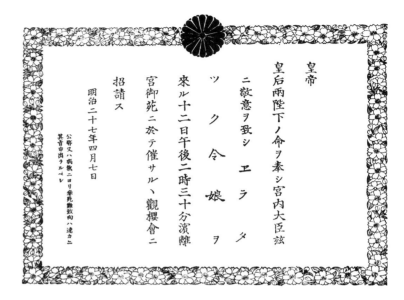

drive past in his carriage, when suddenly my hat was wrenched off my head, and I was pushed forward violently by some heavy hand. On looking round, I saw an officious little policeman glaring at me, my poor hat in his clutches. Not until the procession had disappeared from view could I understand what had happened, but remained meek and hatless. It seems the little man considered my attitude towards his Sovereign was not sufficiently humble, and took this somewhat drastic way of correcting me. I must say this was the only occasion when I have experienced the slightest rudeness or incivility in the streets of a Japanese town, although I do not consider that foreigners are altogether beloved in Japan

Protected by anonymity from any repercussions from this minor act of lese-majesty, Miss Bennett was subsequently invited to accompany her father to another glittering Imperial occasion, a banquet to mark the Silver Wedding Anniversary of the Emperor and Empress:

After passing down endless corridors brilliantly lit with countless candles, along highly polished and very slippery floors, we arrived at the banqueting-hall. I presently found myself sitting with the Chinese Minister, Mr Wong, on my right and a little Japanese Admiral on my left . . . Over five hundred guests were present, seated at long tables, which were exquisitely decorated with orchids, roses, ferns, and every kind of fruit in silver dishes. All the dinner service was also of solid silver.

Miss Bennett's attempts at conversation with her dinner companions met with varying success:

Mr Wong . . . spoke English well . . . He had gorgeous brocades and thick furs lining his long robes. I asked him why he did not wear these brocades outside at night for variety, which idea seemed much to amuse him . . . The little Japanese admiral, who spoke no English, tried to entertain me by making all sorts of figures out of his bread. At each course he asked for a fresh roll, and, by the end of dinner, we had an array of minute bread soldiers, ladies and animals on the table before us, really most cleverly contrived.

The admiral's efforts were apparently more appreciated than the official entertainment:

There was a stage, and some very curious acting was performed – old Japanese plays, with weird Japanese music, which resembled cats on a roof more than anything I have every heard.

The solemnity of the large audience, the weird acting and the appalling music suddenly inspired me with a wild desire to laugh, and I only saved myself from disgrace by bending my head low and trying to think of everything sad I could recollect. It was no use; I was rapidly becoming hysterical, when a kind little Japanese lady, thinking I was feeling faint, offered me her scent-bottle. This restored me to my senses . . .

It is only when writing on the subject of women that Miss Bennett begins to give the impression of being aware that she is out of her depth:

The fair sex in Japan are the most simple and, at the same time, the most complicated creatures imaginable. In their general ideas and knowledge of the world they are like children – delightful children, too – and in their love of enjoyment and simple pleasures they retain their youthful simplicity all their lives.

But, on the other hand, it is almost impossible for a foreigner really to understand their natures. Up to a certain point a Japanese lady is apparently friendly, as she greets one on meeting with that easy grace and courtesy which is one of her peculiar charms. But one seldom becomes more intimate. There seems to be a wall of reserve, beyond which it is impossible to penetrate. I have often attempted to fathom the cause of this barrier, but without success; and I find it is the general experience of those who, like myself, have lived among the Japanese and known them well.

Perhaps the natural antipathy which has long existed between the Eastern and Western races may somewhat account for this want of intimacy; and also, I fear, we Europeans have often wounded the delicate susceptibilities of our Eastern cousins by our want of tact, and our tendency to treat their manners and customs with ridicule, if not contempt.

Miss Bennett's self-awareness is, however, but a passing phase as she soon celebrates the onward march of Western styles and values among her 'almost morbidly sensitive' Japanese sisters:

The social position of Japanese women has very much changed for the better during the last few years, chiefly owing to foreign influence and the spread of Christianity in the country.

The Empress, too, has done much by promoting charitable work of all kinds in the country, and through her influence the horrible custom of blackening the teeth and shaving the eyebrows has been abolished.

But there is evidently still a long way to go:

A Japanese courtship and wedding are both very curious ceremonies, and still somewhat savour of barbarism.

Perhaps the significance of Miss Bennett's opinions can be placed in their proper perspective by her declaration that:

Among all the reminiscences of my life in Japan I think those in which my Chinese chow dog played a part are perhaps the most vivid in my memory.

So much, apparently, for an outbreak of fire in Yokohama, a ten-day trip to the mountains, two Imperial entertainments . . .

Perpetually bedevilling the cultural encounters between Japan and the West was the fact that their notions of culture were themselves so different. Western aesthetes admired the delicacy and humour of intricately carved netsuke *(toggles); they were certainly 'collectable', but were they really art? Literature was to prove an even more problematic sphere. Avant-garde Japanese, eager to demonstrate the richness of their heritage, were horrified to discover that many educated Westerners considered many of their legends and much of their traditional drama either absurd or obscene. Few confronted the problems of literary appreciation more painfully than the novelist Soseki Natsume. His wretched two years on study-leave in London left him mentally scarred for life.*

Soseki had studied in the newly-established Department of English in Japan's most prestigious university, Tokyo, but had found the tuition singularly dull:

In examinations there were such questions as: When was Wordsworth born and when did he die? How many folio editions of Shakespeare's works are there? Write the titles of all the works of Walter Scott in chronological order . . . How could one attain true understanding of literature by answering these questions? . . . After three years of study I could never understand literature.

Having held, in each case rather briefly, a succession of English teaching posts, Soseki was awarded a Ministry of Education grant for two years study in Britain. He arrived in October 1900 with only the vaguest of plans:

The first thing I had to do after landing was to decide where I should stay. I was inclined to go to either Oxford or Cambridge, since they were centres of learning well-known even to us. Fortunately, I had a friend at Cambridge who invited me to visit him. And so I took the opportunity of going there to see what sort of place it was. Besides my friend, I met two or three Japanese there. They were all sons and younger brothers of wealthy merchants, who were prepared to spend thousands of yen per year in order to become 'gentlemen'. My allowance from the government was 1,800 yen a year. In a place where money controlled everything, I could hardly hope to compete with these people . . . I thought: my purpose in coming to England is different from that of these easygoing people; I do not know if the gentlemen of England are so impressive as to make it worth my while to imitate them; besides, having already spent my youth in the Orient, why should I now start learning to conduct myself from these English gentlemen who are younger than I am?

Edinburgh was rejected on the grounds that he would acquire a provincial accent. He settled, therefore, on London but soon became disenchanted with the teaching at University College and shifted to private tuition, though this scarcely made him any happier:

'Essentially an undevotional people . . devotion and ethics, theology and conduct are separate things.'
Basil Hall Chamberlain

The two years I spent in London were the most unpleasant two years of my life. Among English gentlemen, I lived miserably like a lost dog in a pack of wolves.

Soseki became obsessed with his own appearance:

Everyone I see in the street is tall and good-looking. That, first of all, intimidates me, embarrasses me. Sometimes I see an unusually short man, but he is still two inches taller than I am, as I compare his height with mine when we pass each other. Then I see a dwarf coming, a man with an unpleasant complexion – and he happens to be my own reflection in the shop window. I don't know how many times I have laughed at my ugly appearance right in front of myself. Sometimes, I even watched my reflection that laughed as I laughed. And every time that happened, I was impressed by the appropriateness of the term 'yellow race' . . . A few days ago I went out in a frock coat with top-hat, and a couple of working men sneered at me, saying 'a handsome Jap'.

His diary reveals a growing sense of self-contempt:

We are country bumpkins, nincompoop monkeys, good-for-nothing ashen-coloured impenetrable people. So it's natural the Westerners should despise us. Besides, they don't know Japan, nor are they interested in Japan. So even if we deserved their knowledge and respect, there would be no respect or love, as long as they have no time to know us and no eyes to see us.

Soseki's mood might have lightened had his work been going well. But he came to believe that he had set himself a task beyond his capabilities:

On reflection, my knowledge of Chinese classics is not outstanding, yet I can fully appreciate them. My knowledge

of English is not very deep, but it is not inferior to that of Chinese classics. If the same amount of knowledge produces such different results in each subject, it is owing simply to the different natures of each subject. In other words, Chinese literature and English literature are entirely different from each other and cannot be treated as of the same species.

A year after his arrival Soseki tried to warn a friend not to follow his example:

If you want to be a scholar, you should choose a universal subject. English literature will be a thankless task: in Japan or in England, you'll never be able to hold up your head. It's a good lesson for a presumptuous man like me. Study physics.

Soseki's depression went from bad to worse until, according to his landlady, he was:

. . . confining himself in his room for days on end and desperately crying in the dark.

A Japanese friend sent a terse telegram to his sponsors at the Japanese Ministry of Education:

Soseki has gone mad.

Soseki didn't go mad. He went home.

Yoshio Markino, a young Japanese artist, arrived penniless in London in 1897 and for a decade struggled to establish himself until, eventually, he gained some modest prosperity and a reputation as an illustrator. He then wrote an account of his trials in a charmingly idiosyncratic English which the publisher shrewdly allowed to stand uncorrected, believing that this quaintness added to the book's appeal. He was right. A Japanese Artist in

London *went straight into a second edition; and two further books followed. As the author makes clear, despite hardship, he felt much more at home in London than he ever had in California:*

As I had been in America previously for four years, naturally I used to compare everything here with that of America; and what great contrast between the two countries – especially to a Japanese! . . .

I ran away from home to San Francisco in July 1893, with a hope to become a poet or a writer in English. All my friends there advised me to become an artist instead, because one cannot master a foreign language . . . I had to make a livelihood by washing windows and dishes . . .

I was rather amused with my poor life, but by no means did I feel pleasant with the way those Californians treated me. It is a world-known fact that they hate Japanese. While I have been there four years I never went out to the parks, for I was so frightened of those savage people, who threw stones and bricks at me . . . And I was spat on more occasionally. Of course they were very low-class peoples, but even better-class peoples had not a very nice manner to the Japanese. If I got into a tram-car and sat down on an empty seat beside some ladies, they used to glare at me with such disgusting expression, and would get up and go away to find a seat far away from me . . .

Such was my life in America. But I had not so bad a feeling then as I should surely have if it happened now! Because America was the first foreign country I ever visited in my life, so I thought, if we Japanese go out anywhere we shall be treated like that, as an inferior race.

After such experiences I was naturally surprised with the cosmopolitan ideas of the Londoners.

I started my first sight-seeing from Hyde Park and the Green Park and St James's Park. I could not understand all those iron railings. I thought they were to divide private grounds from public ones. But I saw many people on both sides. I so timidly walked inside the rail. Nobody shouted at me. Then I went near the crowds of people with still more fear . . . I waited and waited with beating heart, but nothing happened to me at all. I walked into the crowd who were feeding birds in the lake of St James's Park. Nobody spat on me! I ventured myself into the thickest crowds, and I was squeezed between the peoples. Nobody took any notice of me. 'Hallo, hallo, what's matter?' I said in my heart. 'Perhaps they don't know I am a Japanese.' I took off my hat on purpose to show my black hair. Finally one man pushed me quite accidentally, and he touched his hand to his hat and apologised me very politely. I realised at last that I was in the country where I could enjoy my liberty quite freely. Fancy polite apology instead of swearing and spitting! I felt as if I had come to a paradise in this world . . . Even now, after some thirteen year's stay in London, I often have night-mares of California . . .

At this time I went to a little newspaper shop to buy a box of cigarettes. The shopkeeper treated me quite same way with his countrymen. I asked him if he has seen Japanese before. He said 'No'. Then I asked him again if he was not curious of me? He said, 'No, sir. You see, sir, we 'ave our colonies all hover the world, sir – white men, yellow men, brown men and black men are forming parts of the British nation, so I am not curious of a Japanese gentleman at all.' What a broad mind he had! . . . I made a friendship with him at once, and I told how I was treated in California. He said, 'Thut ain't fair, sir! Indeed, thut ain't fair!' How sweet this word was to me!

The signing of the Anglo-Japanese Alliance in 1902 strengthened British interest in Japan and her people:

It was this time that the Anglo-Japanese alliance was announced. When I was passing that large space near Brixton station several English sailors surrounded me. Evidently they must have been on Japanese water some

'. . . tea and ceremonies are perfectly harmless, which is more than can be affirmed of tea and tattle . . .'
Basil Hall Chamberlain

time for their duty. They began to squeeze out from their head all Japanese words they remembered. As soon as they saw me they shouted, 'Banzai!' (Long Life!), 'Ohayo' (Good Morning), or 'Konnichiwa' (Good Day). One of them started to talk to me, and his beginning word was 'Sayonara' (Good-Bye). I was much amused with their childish innocence. They carried me to a 'Pub' near by and had a drink for our Alliance. I whispered a few words which they might probably have heard from tea-house girls. My anticipation was quite right. They were so delighted, and laughed.

Markino met with much kindness from his various landladies, who fussed over him and, realizing how poor he was, often allowed him to run his rent months in arrears. Even when they were on the friendliest terms, however, they were not reluctant to give him sharp instruction in the 'customs of the country':

Mrs Dryhurst used to give her cook 'holidays' in order to make Japanese dinner. I was the chief cook, and she herself and her daughters and some of her guests were my assistants . . . I was much amused to go out shopping with a little basket. Her grocery was on the corner of the street. But one day I saw a new grocery shop only a few doors beyond. They had such nice fresh mushrooms, and much cheaper . . .

Mrs Dryhurst was so angry with me, and said, 'How dare you go to that new shop! I have been a customer of that old shop since I came to this house. They all know where you come from. You have done such a dreadful thing to me. Yes, I know that a new shop sells better things at a cheaper price. They are advertising themselves just now. You see, after a few weeks they will be just the same as the old shop, if not worse . . .'

Her lecture impressed my heart so much about the English conservative. I am not talking about the political sects now. Let them be Unionists or Liberalists, Nation-alists or Socialists, all the Britons are so Conservative. This is most admirable.

Markino was himself clearly capable of a shrewd appreciation of English society, which he discussed intensely with Japanese student friends. One evening the subject turned to social class and the importance of 'respectability'. Markino's friend suggested that:

. . . the lower-middle class peoples are keeping the highest morals.

Markino set him straight:

They give no annoyance to this world. Perhaps their systematical life gives pleasure to the Government, very much indeed. But, to talk frankly, I think many of them are very artificial, while the highest and the lowest class peoples are natural. The highest peoples are very natural, because they have money enough, and they can do just as they like. The lowest peoples are quite natural as well because they are in despair, and have no hope to elevate their own life. Only the middle-class peoples alone have the ambition to climb up. These sorts of peoples are always thinking not to be cast away from the social life. Perhaps they may meet with great temptation, but they control themselves so well, not for their religious heart, but for the fear that they might lose the next day's bread. Look at the life of clerks. They cannot get their good position unless they have some good references, and to get good references they must 'behave' themselves well . . . I know so many of this class people. They are so timid and so trembling in their daily life as if they are walking on thin ice in order not to be drowned!

There was one aspect of English life of which Markino was especially wary:

'The typical Japanese ceramists were no hired workmen, no mere sordid manufacturers, but artists . . .'
Basil Hall Chamberlain

Only there is one thing I am very cautious about. That is, I am always trying very hard to avoid any business matters with my English friends. They all are very nice to me. But no sooner than I have to do any business with them, I ever so often have been disappointed with them . . .

In Japan we have some unwritten law and invisible spirit which has been overruling all Samurais. This is called Bushido, and sometimes called Yamato Damashi, or the Soul of Old Japan. In England there is an unwritten law and invisible spirit too – I must call it 'The Soul of England'. The Soul of Old Japan is Honour and the soul of England is Business . . . I often notice my English friends change their expression and knock the table with their fists and say, 'Ah, but this is Business.' For 'business' laughter gets serious, drunkards get sober, friends quarrel and lovers depart each other. English husbands would bring their wives to the court, all for the business matter. Of course I know that English peoples do much for Honour also, but in Japan it is only the merchants who do the business, while in England it may even be that Princes have business.

Markino really seems to have 'settled in' in the end:

I am mad in love of London, but it is not at all my curiosity. I have been here long enough. Once I loved London for curiosity: once I was rather homesick. But those periods in my life have passed away a long time ago. Now I love London because I have found out the real art and real comfort in her . . .

But a wistful wariness remained:

I so often meet with the English peoples who express mad admiration of Japan. Of course there are several who really understand everything Japanese, but in a greater majority they make me quite disappointed. May I call those peoples curio-lovers? They love Japan because anything Japanese is strange to their eyes. I am much afraid these peoples shall get tired of Japan sooner or later.

George Rittner's Impressions of Japan, *first published in 1903 and reprinted barely four months later, is a highly opinionated visitor's account which dwells much on the quaint, the charming and the traditional (i.e. children, geisha, drama and bathing), setting these against the background of recent 'rapid and radical' changes. One aspect in particular was of fundamental concern to the author:*

The greatest change of all seemed to have taken place in the country's Art, which twenty years ago was its chief and most distinguishing glory . . . I have tried to show the reasons for . . . deterioration.

Rittner was clearly an enthusiast for what he took to be traditional Japanese taste:

No country in the world is probably so artistic as Japan; the inhabitants from their earliest childhood are taught to love nature, and from that the finest art springs . . .

If you are staying at a tea-house, slide back the paper windows and look out. The sight that presents itself is one not easily to be forgotten – I am taking my picture from a small tea-house at Mogi, near Nagasaki. In front the sea, indescribably blue, a sky with barely a cloud, the gentle sound of an incoming tide, waves splashing against the rocks on which one can see natives sitting contemplating the beauties around them; below the window a garden, small in its dimensions, yet appearing so large, small ponds with goldfish, diminutive bridges spanning model streams a few inches only in breadth, the water running over stones or rocks in imitation of a waterfall, stone *torii* (arches) in front of a toy temple, the whole garden an imitation of a wonderfully laid out park. Turn round again and see the empty room; you cannot help but admire that one *kakemono* (scroll) hanging on the wall, or that one vase of blossoms, because there is nothing else in the room to attract your attention.

An undeniable partisan for the Japanese aesthetic, Rittner yet retains decided European preferences regarding the matter and manner of art, how it shall be produced — and how sold:

In small things the Japanese are wonderfully artistic, no country can paint china better, or carve more perfectly, whether in ivory or wood; but in big things they seem to lose themselves entirely, and flounder trying to imitate what they do not understand. Their own native buildings are ugly, but their imitation of a European house is uglier still.

A Japanese seldom paints or draws from nature. He sees what he wishes to paint, studies it with his eyes, and commits it to memory, before he attempts to put it on paper or silk. Thus paintings on screens, or *kakemonos*, are the work of a few minutes; a few quick flourishes of the brush and the thing is finished. Their ideas of perspective are terrible; a house may as well, according to them, rest on nothing, or be built in the sky, so long as the finished picture is something artistic. They hate being bound by certain laws, whether of perspective or colour. They seldom paint anything with finished lines . . . The Japanese are idealists; they form ideas, and those ideas they reproduce without working upon any fundamental rules. The result may seem to us stiff and unnatural, but it is true to those ideas, though it may not always be true to nature . . .

Paintings by the old Japanese artists cannot be bought; they are as jealously guarded in Japan as the Italian masterpieces are in Italy. What are bought, and bought by the thousands are wonderfully well imitated old kakemonos, so well produced that it would take a connoisseur to tell them from the originals. The gold is made to look several hundred of years old, the silk threads of an embroidery are so carefully worked as to be in places bare, to trick the buyer and induce him to believe he has caught a wonderful bargain . . . The higher the price paid or demanded, the more likely (according to the collector) is the article to be genuine. An American will pay hundreds of pounds (a mere nothing to him) for a piece of Satsuma merely because the clever Japanese salesman has it wrapped in paper, linen, cotton wool, and innumerable boxes lest such a valuable article should be broken. He is duped into buying an apparent imitation because it is so expensive.

But then, in the author's view, Americans get what they deserve:

The Americans, I believe, are chiefly responsible for the decline of Japanese art. They require — and unless they obtain it, will not buy these tawdry articles — a brilliant

'I saw the native home in Japan as a supreme home in Japan as a supreme study in elimination – not only of dirt, but the elimination of the insignificant.'

Frank Lloyd Wright, 1914

'. . cloisonné *with a wealth of ornament, an accuracy of design, a harmony of colour simply miraculous . . .'*
Basil Hall Chamberlain

clash of colouring . . . So far even has their art degraded in the past few years that one is shown an article, palpably, from the very inconsistency of its colouring, a modern piece of manufacture, and told it is hundreds of years old; they will even go so far as to guarantee its age and antiquity by offering written proof showing the temple or noble's house from which it has been un-earthed.

What perhaps Rittner idealizes most is the relationship between art and nature and the place that he feels both have in the lives of the Japanese:

You may walk for miles in Japan and at each bend of the road an effect more striking than the former one will present itself. Should a stream not harmonise with a mountain it will have its course altered; should an inartis-tic tree have the insolence to grow on a hillside covered with mauve and white azaleas it will be cut down by the neighbouring inhabitants. Nothing may look out of place.

A Japanese will sometimes walk miles or climb a mountain to watch a sunset from a particular spot. Imagine an English farmer or a farm labourer, after a day's work, climbing some mountain in Wales to watch a sunset or to obtain a view of some distant landscape. His friends and relations would that evening meet together and con-sult as to what brain specialist he should see . . . they would invent any excuse except the correct one – that his life was empty without some feeling of natural beauty. Few of the poorer people at home can imagine that the soul may require something beyond the ordinary . . . If a nation is artistic, it lives for its art; if a country has no love of art, it must of necessity indulge in some other form of recreation; and too often, I fear, that recreation is found in a public-house or gambling-den, the beginning of the end – man's certain degradation.

Rittner rhapsodizes over Japanese crafts – ceramics, embroidery, cloisonné – but saves his finest praise for one craft above all:

What to my mind is the finest of all arts, I have left till the last. It is better carried out in Japan than in any other country, namely, the gold and cherry lacquer work. No other country can compete with them in this branch of industry. The dampness of the atmosphere is essential to it, and that they have, and so have we, but what we have not, and probably never will have, is sufficient patience. Time with us is too valuable, and the article becomes too expensive for trade purposes.

The article is lacquered over time after time, sometimes twenty times or more, but owing to labour being so cheap in Japan the finished piece of work can be put on the market four times as cheap as if it had been done in Europe, and, I am bound to say, four times as well done.

Rittner's conclusion is an outburst of pure 'Arts and Crafts' propaganda that could have been written by William Morris himself:

A native who does this lacquer work – nearly always a skilled workman, and certainly an artist in the truest sense of the word – gets paid at the rate of from 6d. to 1s. a day, whilst in this country he would get anything from 40s. to 50s. a week. This is the main reason why works of art cannot be manufactured here. The demand is so great and labour so dear that machinery must be used to do the work that human hands, with brains and artistic minds behind them, accomplish in Japan. Does it not stand to reason that an artist must be able to manufacture something more graceful, more natural, and beautiful than a machine can, no matter how wonderfully constructed that machine is or what amount of mechanism it displays? A machine accom-plishes the same work, theoretically, as a modern work-man, and turns it out probably neater, certainly more

Fortune-telling

The official ban on Christianity, brutally enforced for over two centuries, was not formally lifted until some twenty years after the 'opening' of the country. Western missionaries took up the challenge of proselytizing with vigour but found the Japanese far more interested in the technological achievements of their civilization than in its professions of faith.

The fourth edition (1905) of the Church Missionary Society's Japan and the Japan Mission *surveyed the scene in the manner of one chastened by experience:*

There is no doubt whatever that, in the Lord's good time, the religion of Jesus will win a complete victory over the false and unsatisfying superstitions now obtaining in the Empire . . . But it cannot be too well known and realized that we are at present only at the commencement of a struggle the intensity of which it is impossible to exaggerate, and the duration of which it is impossible to forecast.

There has been much too sanguine a view taken by many as to the rapidity with which Japan will become evangelized. This has been due, probably, to too much concentration of thought upon the astonishing results already attained, and to an apparent ignoring of the magnitude of the task still remaining to be accomplished . . . although Christianity can now claim about 150,000 converts (including Roman Catholic and Greek Church, as well as Protestant believers) out of 45,000,000 of inhabitants, as compared with practically none thirty years ago; yet this means . . . nothing more than that . . . nearly 499 out of every 500 persons in the land are still unconverted . . .

We can afford to ignore, as any seriously potent factor in this conflict, the influence of Shintoism and its latest unorthodox but popular development Ten-ri-kyo. The present enlightened Government may well be trusted to discover before long some more sensible and intelligible means of inculcating and fostering patriotism, loyalty, and piety, than the manifestly absurd legends, palpably unhis-

exact and symmetrical, and without a doubt much cheaper, but then I contend that few workmen have any soul in what they are doing . . .

Glance for a moment at Japan and see how different their methods are. Go into a shop where articles of furniture are made, or where wood is carved; each man sits before his panel of wood on which, perhaps, a design is already drawn: in many cases he is even allowed to do that himself, his own imagination is permitted to do what with us only a paid designer is thought capable of doing. What is the result? No imitation; each piece of work different because no two minds are alike. In every piece of work one can trace originality and only because each man is allowed to do that which his soul yearns to do. That is one reason why the man of poorest and humblest parentage can in Japan rise to something higher than the mere labourer or workman. Each man works to attain an end, the highest end it is given a man to aspire to, what his soul asks for – the indulgence of the soul's craving.

torical traditions and grossly superstitious observances of the 'way of the gods'; and, when this has been accomplished successfully, nothing but the dead weight of a defunct cult will have to be dealt with.

But we must weigh well the fact that, although Christianity has met with, and by Divine power already conquered, many – perhaps most – of the false religious systems in the world, still she has never yet in any serious way met, in hand-to-hand combat, at close quarters, that most powerful of all heathen religions, Buddhism. And, in all human probability, the battle will have to be fought out in Japan. The Church does not flinch from the conflict, nor does she doubt her final conquest, but she must be prepared for a struggle such as she has not experienced before, and this, humanly speaking, may be of centuries' duration . . .

But there is, if possible, a still more secure stronghold of the enemy to be attacked . . .

Philosophical speculation has a subtle fascination for the highly intellectual and refined minds of the people . . . These tendencies lead reasonably enough to a general indifference towards supernatural, spiritual verities, and to an acceptance of atheistic and materialistic systems of philosophy; and these, in their turn, develop into unblushing agnosticism or open scepticism as to the necessity or desirableness of any religion whatever . . .

Basil Hall Chamberlain summarized the missionaries' problem briefly and bluntly:

They know also well enough – for every Eastern nation knows it – that our Christian and humanitarian professions are really nothing but bunkum . . . No doubt, individuals may occasionally be met with whose practice carries out their profession. But can any impartial student of history deny that, as nations, the Christian nations (so-called) flout their professions with their deeds?

Herbert G. Ponting, a Fellow of the Royal Geographical Society, prefaces his account of a three-year sojourn In Lotus-Land Japan *with a self-deprecatory apologia:*

When I first went to Japan, my main object was to photograph the country to my heart's content – for my camera has always been, to me, one of the things which made life most worth living. During my travels, however, I took copious notes; and as the fortunes of a wanderer led me several times back again to this beautiful land, these notes became so voluminous that the suggestion of friends, resident in Japan, that I should embody my experiences in a book, written round some of my photographs, was an idea which presented no great difficulty in the way of achievement. Indeed, interesting experiences were so many . . . that the most perplexing problem was what to omit, so as to keep the size of the book within reasonable limits.

In the end Ponting managed to squeeze his reminiscences into 395 pages.

Ponting's preoccupation with photography gives an unusual twist to his interest in Japan and also involved him in a number of minor incidents:

Here [Kyoto] on the 15th May, at the annual festival, horse-races, in which the priests take part, are held . . . and a grand procession of warriors . . . So holy is this procession that no one in the crowd may have his head above another's; and not all the War Office and other official permits I possessed could gain for me the privilege of an elevated position to photograph it. At the very last moment ere the procession arrived I was unceremoniously ousted from the vantage point I had taken up with the permission of the police, who, by thus changing their minds when it was too late for me to prospect for another place, robbed me of a fine chance to secure an interesting picture.

The Japanese 'admire scenes, not scenery.'

Basil Hall Chamberlain

'Buddhism introduced art, introduced medicine, moulded the folk-lore of the country, created its dramatic poetry, deeply influenced politics . . .'

Basil Hall Chamberlain

Negligée is *de rigueur* at Kumamoto in summer-time, and when my Japanese companion sat down to dinner that night his sole and only article of apparel consisted of a loin-cloth. I seized the opportunity to record this interesting phase of native custom by taking two flashlight photographs. This proceeding, it seems, was the cause of much perturbation in Kumamoto town the following day. In order that the smoke from the flashlight might not enter the house I had placed the camera, and fired the powder, on the balcony immediately outside the open *shoji* (paper-screen sliding wall) of the room in which this informal meal was taking place: a report like a pistol-shot accompanied each of the brilliant flashes.

Now it so happened that the balcony faced a river, on the opposite bank of which there lived a journalist . . .

Early next morning we found a number of people on the river banks, closely observing the operations of some dozen men who were digging in the bed of the shallow stream. We also watched for a time, wondering what it all meant, and on enquiry learnt that they were searching for two meteorites which had fallen at that spot the previous evening. They expressed much surprise that we knew nothing about them.

The journalist, it seems, had seen them fall . . . He was directing the digging operations, and spared a few moments to show us an article he had contributed to the daily paper on the subject . . . As my friend finished reading the paragraph to me, and our eyes met, we both burst out laughing, much to the annoyance of the journalist, who was hardly flattered at this unexpected reception of his 'scoop'. We then explained to him how at that precise hour we had made two flashlight photographs on the balcony of the hotel, and that it was, without doubt, these flashes that he had taken for meteors. At this explanation there was a shout of laughter from the assembled observers of the digging operations, and the crestfallen journalist retired, much mortified. . . .

Aso's crater is a truly direful place . . . Occasionally the clouds of vapour that floated up from the great pit parted, and we could see the crater bottom, with its thousand cracks and fissures, from which the stream hissed and roared . . . Once the wind veered for a few moments and we were quickly enveloped in the steam, which sent us running, sliding and tumbling to get away from the suffocating fumes that gripped us in the throat and set up paroxysms of coughing . . . For the benefit of those of photographic predilections who read these lines I would offer a few remarks about these fumes . . . On my first visit to the mountain I took with me a number of isochromatic, as well as ordinary plates . . . All the isochromatic plates were completely ruined by being exposed to the sulphurous fumes, which it seems attacked the silver in the film. Never having used such plates on a volcano before, I had no idea that anything wrong had happened, and after descending the mountain I went on exposing these plates for the next two days . . . Months later, when I came to develop the plates in California, I was completely nonplussed to account for the extraordinary manner in which the latent image came out. The films were covered with blotches, and when the negatives were dry, parts of them were positive. They were perfectly useless, and it was only when I remembered that these plates had been subjected to Aso-san's sulphurous vapours that I was able to account for the occurrence. The ordinary plates, strange to see, were not affected in any way whatever.

Those who know what it means to make an expensive journey in order to secure photographic results, and then to find that plates of splendid subjects – which one may never have a chance of getting again – have been ruined by accident, will understand my feelings when I realised what my thoughtlessness had cost me. I therefore offer my experience as a warning to others never to allow their plates to be exposed to the action of sulphurous fumes.

Summer negligée at Kumamoto

It wasn't always the technology that was bothersome, as Ponting discovered when Mount Asama suddenly threw up a massive column of smoke and steam:

Here was a wonderful chance to secure a unique photograph, but on looking round for the coolies I saw them madly rushing down the mountain-side with my cameras as fast as legs could carry them. Realising that if I did not stop them I should miss the chance of a lifetime to get a picture at the lip of a volcano in a state of violent activity, I ran after them, calling to them to stop. The guide shouted back that we should all be killed if we did, and they continued their rush down the mountain-side faster than ever . . . Failing to check them with my shouts, I went after them, and, being unencumbered, soon overhauled the man with my hand-camera; but he was half-crazed with fear, and not all my entreaties could make him slack his pace. Seeing the chance of a unique picture slipping away – for I knew the best smoke effects would soon be over – I was reluctantly compelled to use a more forcible method, which had the desired effect. Quickly unlashing the camera from his pack, I returned with another and older coolie, who had stopped at my bidding, to the crater's lip, and there hastily took a snapshot showing Hurley and his camera near the brink, with the smoke pouring out of the crater in the background . . .

When all danger was over, the coolies, who were busy haranguing the guide half a mile away, returned, and I could see they meant to make trouble. The guide angrily demanded to know what I meant 'by striking a man who was running away to save his life.'

Seeing that all danger was over before I had started in pursuit, it seemed to me he had scarcely stated the case quite fairly; but I knew that in Japan it was a very serious offence to handle a man roughly, even though I had been gentler than the circumstances might have warranted, and I knew, too, that I should surely get into trouble unless I

could turn the tables on them. I therefore simulated all the wrath I could, and demanded in turn to know what they meant by shirking the work I was paying them liberally to do, and running away with my apparatus when the time came for me to use it. I denounced them as cowards unworthy of the name of Japanese, whom I had hitherto supposed to be a courageous people able to look death in the face without flinching; but that henceforth I should look upon them as poltroons who could be frightened out of their lives by a little smoke and a few stones flying in the air. How could they ever expect to beat the Russians in the coming war if this was all the spirit and courage they could show? I added that I should report their conduct to the hotel proprietor as soon as we got back, and advise him never to let such men accompany any foreign visitors again.

The guide's face was a study as I delivered this oration. He was completely nonplussed, and when I had finished he veered round, and instead of pouring the vials of his wrath on my head, vented it on the coolies. He hotly denounced them, as I had done, quite overlooking the fact that I had included him in my impeachment as being the worst of the lot, for he had nothing whatever to carry, and had outstripped all the others in his flight for safety. At his change of front the coolies hung their heads in shame, and then came to me, pleading forgiveness, and begging that I would say nothing of the matter at the hotel. This I agreed to, and rewarded the old man, who had stood by me, with a substantial tip, then and there, much to his satisfaction. It is interesting to add that the camera-carrier, whom I had reluctantly treated so unceremoniously, was indefatigable in my interests during the rest of my stay . . .

Nor was this the only occasion on which Ponting was able to reverse a misfortune to his advantage:

I had set up my camera by the moat (of Osaka castle) . . . when I noticed some soldiers watching me from the

Photographing the crater's lip at Aso-San

walls. They disappeared and came back again with some more; then they all retreated from view. Just afterwards I saw a commotion by the drawbridge; an officer and a number of men engaged in a discussion were carefully observing me. The officer then gave some instructions, and a squad of men marched over the bridge and along the moat-side in my direction. When they reached me, one of them, who spoke excellent English, thus addressed me:

'You must excuse me, but I must arrest you. It is forbidden to sketch the castle.' I therefore excused him and submitted to the inevitable, and was conducted, camera, cases, and all, into the castle. There I was given to understand by a sergeant that I had committed a serious offence . . . and on my War Office permits being examined it was pointed out that although many other fortified areas were included in my permission to use a camera, Osaka was omitted. As Osaka is only a garrison town and possesses no fortifications, I had not thought it necessary to stipulate for it in my request for the privilege of photographing. I explained this to my interrogator. He had, however, no power to release me until another officer came, and I was detained in the guard-room for several hours – the butt for the wit of the men, whose veneer of courtesy quickly rubbed off when they found they had the whip-hand of a foreigner for the time being.

Finally an officer, quite a young man, arrived and cross-examined me. After asking my name and nationality – both of which were clearly defined in my permit – he demanded to know if I were a Russian. On my assuring him that I was not, and that my country was stated in the document which I had handed him, he asked me, 'Are you quite sure you are not Russian?' I told him there was no shadow of doubt in my mind on the point; but this did not seem to convince him, for he plied the further question, 'Who is your father?' Becoming a little nettled at such vacuous interrogations, I replied that he was the son of my grandfather . . . and that I did not consider it necessary to draw him into the business at all . . . After admonishing me, as he might have scolded a child, he graciously permitted me to go. In an hour I returned to the castle, and, handing my card to the sergeant of the guard, requested him to send it in to the Commandant. This he did, and I had the pleasure of being received and entertained with wine and cigars, and afterwards being shown all over the castle enclosure by the courteous old gentleman, much to the chagrin of the lieutenant who had questioned me so ridiculously, and who, it seemed, was the Commandant's aide-de-camp. Japan is no exception to other countries in respect of the officiousness sometimes assumed by underlings.

It seems not to have occurred to Ponting, however, that had he followed correct form and presented his card in the first place the entire incident might never have happened.

Enthusiasm in Britain for 'Things Japanese' reached a peak in the decade after the signing of the Anglo-Japanese Alliance in 1902. Japan's hard-fought victory over the Russians in 1904–5 was widely applauded. The Times, *noting general European astonishment at the defeat of a European power by an Asian state, took the opportunity to pontificate:*

That is the trouble at the root of the present situation – the past inability of the West to take Japan seriously . . . All this is due to the superficial study of Japan which has characterised Western contact with it. We as a nation alone appear to have formed a shrewder estimate of the Power which had in Eastern waters a naval strength superior to our own, and which at a pinch can put half-a-million men into the field. But for the rest, they still were pleased to look upon the Japanese through the eyes of the aesthetic penman, and thought of the nation as a people of pretty dolls dressed in flowered silks and dwelling in paper houses . . . The professional guide and the tourist are

'This astonishing people is the only one in Asia that has never been conquered and appears to be unconquerable . . .'
Encyclopedie, 1751

responsible for much – they are responsible for the ficti-
tious picture which caricatured Japan . . .

*In 1906 Prince Arthur of Connaught headed a British mission to
confer the Order of the Garter on the Emperor Meiji. In 1908 the
same luminary became president of a committee to organize an
exhibition which would, as the Japanese side felicitously put it,
represent 'Nichi-Ei domei no hana' (the flowering of the Anglo-
Japanese Alliance). The site chosen for the exhibition was at
Sheperd's Bush, to the west of central London, where Britain had
hosted the 1908 Olympics and staged a great Anglo-French
'exposition'. Former British consul Longford assured readers of*
Nineteenth Century and After *that they were in for something
special from the Japanese:*

Nothing that she has hitherto done approaches in extent
and completeness the attempt which she is now making to
afford to Europeans an opportunity of studying not only
her art and industries, her economic development and her
progress in modern civilization . . . but her national
history from the earliest days . . .

*When the exhibition opened in May 1910 the poet and critic
Lawrence Binyon endorsed Longford's prediction with an
enthusiasm bordering on ecstasy:*

I wonder if the English public appreciates the extraordinary compliment which Japan has paid it . . . Japanese
collectors have sent us treasures quite beyond price . . .
What the traveller to Japan never sees, things hidden away
in the temples or in the 'godowns' (warehouses) of the
great amateurs, is here in London for all of us to feast on.
    Every day . . . the watchful visitor will note some little
change: a scroll painting is unrolled to show another
portion of its length, or one of the marvellous old swords,
sheathed yesterday, will today be gleaming bare. As this
first instalment may be withdrawn at least, next week, I

would counsel all lovers of beautiful art not to put off their
first visit and to make their visits frequent. It is a chance
that will never occur again.

*One object in particular fired Binyon's ardour; appropriately
enough it was a* namban *('southern barbarian') screen, the
product of the earliest phase of European encounters with Japan:*

Here is something of a kind that no other art in the world
can show. The impression at a distance is of a minutely
variegated pattern, intricate in line and chequered with
rich, clean colour invaded by rivulets of gold, decorative,
but by no means tamely so, for the whole design vibrates
with movement. At a nearer view we see that we are
looking on a vivid and multitudinous scene packed with
human interest. It is a great city festival, with troops of
swirling dancers and stage performances and thronging
spectators. We are looking at this peopled space from
above through patches of broken cloud; in the rents of the
gold appear now green pines and now a crimson roof and
now excited faces and bodies in eager motion. Right in the
midst of the crowd is a group of Europeans in ruffs – it is
the beginning of the seventeenth century – talking and
gesticulating. And all this vehement animation is
combined with the most audaciously conventional scheme
to produce a triumphantly decorative effect.

The critic of The Athenaeum *was less rapturous but made the
telling point that the very style and staging of the exhibition was
as significant as what it contained:*

There is little among the contemporary work shown . . .
to give the lie to the current opinion that contact with
Western civilization has ruined a national tradition without
satisfactorily replacing it . . . In the paintings, as amongst
the sculpture, there is a tendency for the earliest work to be
the finest . . .

It would be taking a narrow view, of course, to measure the artistic importance of this exhibition by its Art Section alone. The fact that with this race the artistic impulse is the rule . . . makes this contact with them important, even if it comes at a time when they have passed their highest point of artistic culture. We may be inclined to flatter the productions of the Japanese craftsmen in the exhibition because the workmen are themselves picturesque, but we saw some pottery painting done at one of the stalls which reached a high level of artistry. The ingenious woodwork about the exhibition, the architectural models, the perfectly delightful dolls, are works of art in themselves. We confess to a hope that the organizers of . . . great exhibitions . . . may catch from their momentary partners something of their confident belief in the attractive power of beauty . . . For example, one of the approaches to the exhibition is now made through a representation by the scene-painter's art of the four seasons in Japan. There is nothing essentially Japanese in the art displayed – it could be done just as well by English artists; but the approach . . . which on many similar occasions has been a nightmare of insistent advertisements becomes a pleasurable entertainment consecutively developed, without a dull moment . . . we believe that the confidence of the Japanese organizers of the present exhibition is . . . well founded. It would be no small achievement if we could convince their English colleagues that the British public is not artistically blind or wholly unresponsive.

Other exhibits included Japanese gardens, a tea-house, 'authentic villages' peopled by Ainu and Taiwanese and a regimental band. There were also some two thousand private exhibitors representing trade and industry. By the time the exhibition closed in October it had received six million visitors in only six months, more than any other exhibition since the Great Exhibition of 1851.

In 1912 the Emperor Meiji died. The continuing closeness of Anglo-Japanese relations was symbolized by the presence in his funeral procession of five hundred British sailors, the only occasion in history in which foreign troops have participated in Japanese Imperial rites. Prince Arthur of Connaught recorded the occasion as 'a weird and impressive sight.' During the First World War Japan supplied both naval and humanitarian support to Britain and was acknowledged by Foreign Secretary, A.J. Balfour, as:

. . . a faithful ally, who rendered us valuable assistance in an hour of serious and very critical need . . .

The post-war world, however, required a new diplomatic order and the era of alliance ended as delegations met in Washington to organize a new security framework for the Pacific. While they did so, Britain and Japan, as if to re-affirm old ties, exchanged royal visits. In 1921 Crown Prince Hirohito made a three-week tour of Britain. In 1922 it was the turn of the Prince of Wales:

No Western power ever received a foreign prince with greater enthusiasm than was shown by the Japanese people everywhere during this visit. The warmth of his welcome was almost overpowering. A nation that until only a little while before had looked upon cheering as an insult, and dead silence as the only proper way of saluting royalty, literally shouted itself hoarse . . . It might well be said that the Prince was carried across Japan on a torrent of cheers . . . Here was the voice of the East heard in no uncertain tones, giving vent in a Western way to its friendship and admiration for the nation's guest. The Prince is not likely to forget his progress from the quayside at Yokohama through four weeks of lavish hospitality. . . .

The journey from Yokohama to Tokio took him through crowds that were practically continuous along a route 19 miles in length . . . All the workers left the dockyards and factories to see him; the trams stood still,

A cloisonné *vase for the emperor*

The Prince of Wales and the Prince Regent of Japan

The Prince of Wales and his staff in kimonos – a gift from Prince Regent Hirohito. Lt. Louis Mountbatten stands at the extreme left of the back row

and even the priests came from their temples to stand beside the railway with heads bent and eyes fixed reverently on the ground. The noise died away as the train entered Tokio central station, where the Prince Regent awaited his guest in solemn silence . . . Once clear of the station, however, his Royal Highness was once again overwhelmed by the cries of the people . . . he had a reception that could not be surpassed.

The first week was spent in the capital, and was devoted almost entirely to official functions, performed in accordance with the rigid etiquette of the Imperial Court . . . a series of state banquets, garden parties and receptions, and visits to public institutions . . . The morning after his arrival he drove . . . to the University, where the students and the faculty were assembled in a pavilion in the grounds to see him presented with an address of welcome. After lunch, he was called to the balcony of Akasaka palace to hear 2,000 little boys and girls sing 'God Save the King' in English, and to make them a little speech. On Good Friday he attended service at the Anglican church, and unveiled two tablets to the memory of former members of the British colony killed in the war. He saw the pick of the Japanese army at Yoyogi parade ground, in the suburbs of Tokio, where he reviewed a complete division of the Imperial Guard. On this occasion he wore the uniform of a Japanese general . . . He spent one morning at the Peace Exhibition, viewing the many industrial, commercial, and artistic exhibits . . . Another public appearance was in Hibiya Park . . . where 15,000 students greeted him with enthusiasm.

The entertainments given in his honour involved much labour and more expense. Two of the Prince's hosts thought nothing of building private theatres, solely for a single after-dinner performance. Count Uchida, the Foreign Minister, added a wing to the Foreign Office residence . . . The performers were artistes of the highest merit, and they were paid for two months solely to ensure

their attendance on this occasion. Baron Mitsui, one of the richest men in the world, put up a theatre in the courtyard of his Japanese mansion, which cost £30,000 . . .

This gala performance at the Imperial Opera House gave his Royal Highness an even more comprehensive view of the Japanese stage. So keen was the competition among the leading actors to appear on this occasion, that a programme lasting until after one o'clock in the morning was fully carried out, in order that as great a number of performers as possible might be included . . .

Two garden parties gave further opportunities for the Prince to meet the distinguished men of the Empire. The Imperial cherry blossom garden party . . . was held in the park of Shinjoku palace . . . More than 9,000 guests were bidden to this gathering . . . The Marquis Inouye gave a garden party in the grounds of his delightful residence . . . Admiral Togo, the greatest hero of Japan, was the dominant figure . . . He always stood apart from the other guests, a silent, shy, little man in naval uniform, his eyes fixed meekly on the ground, and only looking up when someone was brought foward and presented. He smiled on one occasion when an English guest told him that in England he was called 'the Nelson of Japan'. Admiral Togo shook his head deprecatingly and continued to study the pattern of the lawn. The Marquis Inouye provided many diversions for his guests. He engaged famous artists and decorators of pottery to prepare souvenirs on the spot . . . A large temporary building was erected adjoining the wonderful rock garden solely for the service of refreshments . . .

One day was spent at Yokohama. His Royal Highness unveiled the Allied War Memorial in the General Cemetery, for which ceremony a guard was landed from the *Renown* . . . This honour was deeply appreciated by the British community, for ordinarily no foreign troops are permitted to bear arms in Japanese territory . . .

When the Prince left Tokio for the interior, he found

The Prince of Wales meets Admiral Togo – the 'Nelson of Japan'

everywhere the same fervent enthusiasm. He travelled first to Nikko, celebrated for its beautiful temples, and the usual outpouring of villages marked the progress of his special train. Happy school children were collected in thousands at every wayside station; the mayor was there in a frock coat, supported by all the municipal officials and flanked by rows upon rows of smiling women in their best kimonos; workers from the fields and prosperous factory owners at the head of their employees; Shinto priests; Buddhist priests; Christian missionaries leading the cheers of the mission schools; ex-soldiers and prefectural authorities . . . Such receptions never grew monotonous. Four days were spent in the Hakone lake district, where the Prince had many varied views of the beautiful mountain Fuji-yama . . . He met the Prince Regent for the last time at a palace over-looking Lake Hakone . . . before continuing his journey to Western Japan . . . He visited the Fujiya hotel, which . . . rocked ominously in the earthquake of April 25, when considerable damage was done in Tokio. The Prince regretted that he did not experience the shock. He was motoring . . . at the time and knew nothing of it until afterward.

A week in and around Kyoto revealed the charm of old Japan . . . Kyoto shows the effect of western civilisation less than other large cities of Japan. Its ancient monuments are carefully preserved and the modern skyscraper type of office building which disfigures Tokio has not yet appeared. . . .

Then came an abrupt transition from ancient to modern Japan. The Prince left Nara by tram, and an hour later entered Osaka, the bustling industrial centre which has been called the 'Japanese Birmingham' – a city of mills and factories overhung with smoke, altogether progressive, prosperous and unlovely. The Royal visit lasted barely two hours, but the enthusiasm of Osaka's workpeople made it a memorable two hours. They surged around the Prince and ignored all efforts of the police to keep him at a distance; they followed him madly, shouting like an English football crowd . . .

The voyage through the Inland Sea gave his Royal Highness a last look at rural Japan, and at places yet untouched by Western 'progress' . . . Flat-bottomed fishing-boats ventured as near the steamer as possible, that their quaintly garbed crews might salute the Prince; British and Japanese flags flew from their masts and on every face was a smile. Sometimes a large schooner would put off with the entire population of a village on board, the school children packed tightly at the bows, the women amidships, and the men astern and clinging to the rigging . . .

While at Takamatsu, his Royal Highness was the guest of Count Matsudaira . . . (who) . . . spent more than £10,000 in preparing for this half- day visit . . . More than three hundred servants were busy for a week preparing the dinner and the decorations . . . Twelve geishas, wearing silk kimonos especially woven for the occasion, in which Union Jacks and the Rising Sun were intermingled, gave a graceful dance peculiar to the province.

Next . . . afternoon (the steamer) anchored off the sacred island of Miyajima . . . After visiting the temples, the Prince spent some time buying souvenirs . . . The *Keifuku Maru* that night appeared to rest in a vast field covered with coloured flowers. Thousands of paper lanterns, each supported on a wooden base, were set afloat from the far shore and they drifted slowly across the windless bay until the placid surface was hidden under a mantle of glowing scarlet and green and orange. One could not have believed that such a beautiful effect could be secured with such simple, inexpensive materials.

After seeing Miyajima, the Prince spent a day with the Japanese Navy. He first travelled . . . to the island of Etajima, to visit the Naval Academy – the Osborne of Japan . . . From Etajima . . . to Kure, the great naval port and dockyard . . . After luncheon there, his Royal Highness went over the dockyard establishment. He saw object lessons in disarmament, inspired by the Washington Conference, which his hosts pointed out with mournful pride . . . He was told that 40 per cent of the dockyard personnel would have to be discharged . . . The Prince re-embarked in the *Renown* in the afternoon and sailed for Kagoshima, the last port of call . . . For the last time he faced the deafening tumult of a Japanese crowd . . . After lunch at Prince Shimadzu's villa, a company of archers in the traditional dress of Samurai, showed their skill . . . The Prince drove back to the harbour at 3 o'clock and found it packed . . . School children had the place of honour . . . There must have been 8,000 of them . . . Admiral Togo visited the *Renown* half an hour later, as did members of the Prince's Japanese suite, to shake hands and receive his thanks for the nation's wonderful welcome. When the *Renown* steamed out of the harbour . . . small craft of all kinds surrounded her with volleys of 'Banzais' . . . From his saluting platform, the Prince watched a very inspiring scene as the crowded quays slowly melted in the mist, and the voice of Japan came fainter and fainter across the water. Two hours later he went back to his post above the bridge. The wind had risen and rain drove in gusts against the *Renown* . . . Her forward turrets and forecastle were hidden by bluejackets massed with their faces to starboard, as the (Japanese escort) cruisers ahead swung aside and turned back. On they came in the twilight, so close that their crews could be seen standing at attention. The *Renown's* bands played 'Auld Lang Syne', and from the passing ships came cheer after cheer, as caps were raised high in the air. Cheer answered cheer, and the Prince, bareheaded in the rain, waved his hand. . . .

The cruisers disappeared, steaming again towards Kagoshima, and the *Renown* made her course for the open sea . . .

FURTHER READING

The themes of this book have been the subject of a number of academic studies, including:

Beasley, W.G., *Great Britain and the Opening of Japan 1834–1858* (1951).

Bowers, John Z., *Western Medical Pioneers in Feudal Japan (1970)*.

Checkland, Olive, *Britain's Encounter With Meiji Japan 1868–1912* (1989).

Conte-Helm, Marie, *Japan and the North-East of England: From 1862 to the Present Day* (1989).

Fox, Grace, *Britain and Japan 1858–1883* (1969).

Irie, Akira (ed.), *Mutual Images: Essays in American – Japanese Relations* (1975).

Jones, Hazel J., *Live Machines: Hired Foreigners and Meiji Japan* (1980).

Lehmann, Jean-Pierre, *The Image of Japan: From Feudal Isolation to World Power 1850–1905* (1978).

Nish, Ian H., *The Anglo-Japanese Alliance: The Diplomacy of Two Island Empires* (1985).

Paske-Smith, M., *Western Barbarians in Japan and Formosa in Tokugawa Days 1603–1868* (1930).

Sansom, Sir George, *The Western World and Japan: A Study in the Interaction of European and Asiatic Cultures* (1950).

Yokoyama, Toshio, *Japan in the Victorian Mind: A Study of Stereotyped Images of a Nation 1850–80* (1987).

The following titles are written with the general reader more in mind:

Barr, Pat, *The Coming of the Barbarians: A Story of Western Settlement in Japan 1853–1870* (1967).

Barr, Pat, *The Deer Cry Pavilion: A Story of Westerners in Japan 1868–1905* (1968).

Cortazzi, Hugh, *Victorians in Japan: In and around the Treaty Ports* (1987).

Williams, Harold S., *Tales of Foreign Settlements in Japan* (1958).

Williams, Harold S., *Foreigners in Mikadoland* (1963).

For studies of significant individual characters see:

Barr, Pat, *A Curious Life for a Lady: the story of Isabella Bird* (1970).

Beauchamp, Edward R., *An American Teacher in Early Meiji Japan* (1976), on W.E. Griffis.

Blacker, Carmen, *The Japanese Enlightenment: A Study of the Writings of Fukuzawa Yukichi* (1964).

Cortazzi, Hugh (ed.), *A Diplomat's Wife in Japan; Sketches at the turn of the century by Mary Crawford* (1982).

Cortazzi, Hugh, *Dr. Willis in Japan 1862–1877: British Medical Pioneer* (1985).

Cortazzi, Hugh (ed.), *Mitford's Japan: The Memoirs and recollections 1866–1906 of Algernon Bertram Mitford, First Lord Redesdale* (1985).

Cortazzi, Hugh, and Webb, George, *Kipling's Japan: Collected Writings* (1988).

Herbert-Gustar, L.K., and Nott, P.A., *John Milne, Father of Modern Seismology* (1980).

Manthorpe, Victoria, (ed.), *The Japan Diaries of Richard Gordon Smith* (1986).

McWilliams, Vera, *Lafcadio Hearn* (1946).

Tames, Richard, *Servant of the Shogun: A Biography of William Adams, the first Englishman in Japan* (1981).

Whitney, C.A.W., *Clara's Diary: An American Girl in Meiji Japan* (1979).

Several of the 'classic' contemporary accounts of Meiji Japan have been re-issued in modern reprints:

Becker, J.E. de, *The Nightless City or the History of the Yoshiwara Yukwaku* (1971). An early exposé of the 'entertainment' business in Japan's pleasure districts.

Black, John R., *Young Japan: Yokohama and Yedo 1859–79* (1968). Black, an Australian, was a pioneer of modern journalism in Japan and a fierce critic of British officialdom.

Chamberlain, Basil Hall, *Things Japanese* (1971). First published in 1894, this witty and informative dictionary-style pocket encyclopedia went through half a dozen editions in a decade. It is still a gem and a delight.

Preble, Lt. G.H., *The Opening of Japan* (1962). A personal account by one of Perry's officers and therefore a useful corrective to the officially approved history of the expedition.

Satow, Sir Ernest, *A Diplomat in Japan. The inner history of the critical years in the evolution of Japan when the ports were opened and the monarchy restored* (1968). Satow was the first British diplomat to achieve a real mastery of the Japanese language, which he used to play a significant 'under-cover' role in the intrigues surrounding the 'Meiji Restoration' of 1868.

INDEX